The Complete Book of
SOFTBALL

A publication of
Leisure Press.
597 Fifth Avenue; New York, N.Y. 10017

Library of Congress Catalog Card Number: 83-80707

ISBN: 0-88011-212-3

Cover design: Bill Wilkens
Cover photo: David Madison
Book design: Brian Groppe
Production: Robin Terra

The Complete Book of
SOFTBALL

Robert G. Meyer, Ph.D.

*The Loonies' Guide
to Playing and
Enjoying the Game*

LEISURE PRESS

NEW YORK

To the Wild Bunch—
Chris, Mary, John, Andy, Sarah, and Monika

and

To the original Loonies and to all
who are true Loonies at heart

Contents

Preface

"Softball" ludo, ergo sum
I play softball, therefore I am
   Rene Descartes
   1596-1650
   Discours de la Méthode

Softball is a game that I have enjoyed playing since boyhood, both fast and slow pitch; industrial, church, and city leagues; and maybe the most fun of all, pick-up games at playgrounds and parks. I've coached and/or managed both children and adults, and men and women (but confess I enjoy playing the game more). Maybe it was all of the fun that I had playing, that allowed me to have some fun writing this book. Just finding the many quotes from the great and famous who have commented on their love of softball throughout the ages was a real delight (I'll confess I may have ever so slightly changed at least a couple of these quotes).

   I wrote this book because my own perception was that most softball books have a very technical how-to approach to the game, while others focus almost exclusively on enjoyment and/or historical aspects. I feel that the present book thoroughly covers the technical detail issues, but hopefully preserves the spirit of enjoyment that truly makes the game worthwhile. Since Bill Plummer III, Director of Communications at the Amateur Softball Association, provided the great majority of material on the history of the game and the game as it is today, I know that we have that well covered. In addition, I've included material that I've seen nowhere else in regard to softball, i.e. the section on playing the game better. This last section integrates information on weight training, training exercises, imagery training and vision and concentration training, with data and ideas from the field of sports psychology. The direct application is of course to softball, but most readers will find that the material in this section will be useful in virtually all sports, and expecially in other ball sports.

   As a result, this book can hopefully provide both greater enjoyment and better skills to virtually any player, no matter what their age or level of experience. In fact, many of the very best players athletically have not mastered at least some of the fundamentals, and very few at any level have been introduced to the material in section three on playing the game better.

In any endeavor like this, many people help out. A great thanks goes first of all to Bill Plummer III, and to the Amateur Softball Association. Not only was Bill most helpful with his excellent contribution on the history of the game, but he and Don Porter and the fine staff at ASA provided photos, statistics, and much needed guidance and encouragement throughout the development of this book.

A special note of appreciation goes to Dr. James Peterson and the staff at Leisure Press, who allowed it all to happen; and also to Bill Barke, my editor at Allyn and Bacon, who gave me my first shot at professional writing in the area of psychology.

I am very grateful to Mike Moll and Ken McNiel, who are both Loonies and fine coaches and softball players as well, as they provided important contributions and critiques throughout the section on how to play the game. Jim McGovern and Paul Salmon also provided good critiques; Paul in addition supplied several fine photos. Ed Herzer and Michele Ising supplied the line art. Phil Johnson and Steve Krawiec, both of whom are dedicated weight trainers and psychologists, gave much help in the chapter on physical training methods. Critical organizational and clerical support were provided first and foremost by Donna Smith and Kathleen McDaniel, and also by Suzanne Paris, Sharon Mills, Tammy Smith, and Sara Biagton.

*I did not want to become the
creature it could so easily
turn me into. I did not want
to release my grasp on pride
and fall into the blind arena
of softball compulsion.*
John MacDonald
Area of Suspicion (1961)

1

An Introduction To The Game

The Delight of the Game

Breathes there the man, with soul so dead
who never to himself hath said
I love a good softball game
Sir Walter Scott
(1771-1832)
The Lay of the Last Minstrel

There are good reasons why softballers can lay claim to playing the truly American team sport. First, as detailed later, the sport was born in the heartland of America, probably in Chicago, or at least somewhere in the upper Midwest. Secondly, though it depends on whose statistics you pay attention to, it is arguably the most popular team sport in America. The only team sport that might legitimately lay claim to more participants is bowling, and bowling is hardly a team sport in the true sense of that word. The team's score in bowling is a simple summation of individual performances. In softball, the team's performance is a blending, a team effort throughout.

The range of participants in softball is as democratic as the American dream. It's a game loved by factory workers, attorneys, waitresses, executives, movie stars, clerks, senators, drunks and dope fiends, and even a President or two. People of all ages play it; people of superb skills and people of indefinite or undiscovered athletic ability likewise indulge. There are no social, sexual, or ethnic barriers; in fact, it is one of the very few team sports where the idea of coed teams can truly work without much strain. The number of women's softball teams has risen markedly in the last decade. While approximately 10,000 young women formally participated in softball at the high school level in 1971-72, approximately 165,000 did so in 1978-79, and the number has been increasing just as rapidly since then.

Consensus estimates are that more than 30,000,000 Americans play softball every year, around 20,000,000 of these on *organized* teams. Americans abroad, such as armed forces personnel, have introduced the game into many countries, and more than 10,000,000 persons in these countries also play the game.

The Lord prefers softball players.
That is why he makes so many of them.
Abraham Lincoln
(1809-1865)
J. Morgan
Our President

Why Do They Play It?

Actually, there are many good reasons for playing softball. However, I do think that the following set of reasons, as quoted by Arthur Noren (1947) from a promotional bulletin put out by a staff of the Intramural Sports Department of the University of Michigan during the 1940's, is maybe stretching it just a bit. They say:

"It is a health contributing and invigorating game; one that presents numerous educational possibilities, and one that offers untold recreational and social advantages (and) has no outstanding hazards. It is a scientific game demanding the use of mental alertness as well as physical skill; it allows individual skill and yet instills cooperation; calls for judgment and quick thinking; it develops coordination; and it permits action for all players at almost all times.

From a community standpoint the game has real merit, for in our many leagues, classified as sandlot, playground, interscholastic, industrial, church, minor and major city, players of all nationalities, of all strata of civic life, are brought together...the game is interesting not only to the players but also to the spectators...finally, softball has a real carryover value, for informal games may be organized at outings and picnics, and almost every city with a recreational program will want to include softball for adults as well as for the younger groups. It can be played successfully for a much longer period in life than can regulation baseball."

From reading the above, one might assume that softball mixes the values of Geritol, psychotherapy, the Junior Chamber of Commerce, and old snake oil cures into one panacea for the ills of modern society. Of course, this is not the case. Realistically, the game is hardly invigorating in the same sense that handball, jogging, or swimming are. On the other hand it's probably a cut above golf. There's also some question whether 'it's a scientific game. In the many softball games that I gave seen there has been little science in evidence. Also, some of the community goals don't always seem to be reached.

I am reminded of one game in which I was pitching in which community spirit was probably decreased rather than increased. Probably because of the closeness of the game and humidity of the night, some good natured bantering had gradually taken on an edge of hostility as the game progressed into the late innings. Our team was well ahead, which surprised us as much as it did the opposition. In the last inning, a young man of exceedingly fair complexion hit a high pop-up and, though out, he trotted around the bases. In doing so he passed by a couple of our"fringe fans" who were leaning over the fence behind our dugout. They had to lean since they had been detained at several local watering holes on their way to the ballgame. As the fair haired one (who was also a bit obnoxious himself) passed by, one of these fellows slurred the comment, "Hey, you wierd albino, why don't you try to hit them straight out instead of straight up in the air." The fair haired one had undoubtedly heard many similar derogatory comments over the years, and he decided that he had had enough. He leapt over the fence and proceeded to sober up our fringe fan through the diligent administration of physical punishment. Players from both teams apparently felt that they were missing out in this community event and quickly joined in.

My own feeling is that one should look elsewhere for any high level of development of science, community renewal, or physical prowess. But, what is experienced is quite simply fun, competitiveness, relaxing enjoyment, and a sense of a timeless sport that one can participate in from youth even into old age.

Also, as in all games, there is the magic of losing oneself in the game, of experiencing Moments of Magic when cares, regrets, and worries fall away and the self becomes just a part of the game. And since almost anyone can play, almost anyone can share in the magic. Maybe we even return to it sometimes for reasons analogous to those given by the French poet Jean Cocteau for using heroin: "Everything that we do in life, including love and playing softball is done in an express train traveling towards death. To smoke opium is to leave the train while in motion. It is to be interested in something other than life and death."

For some players it even becomes this compelling. As a player commented in an article called "The Glory Boys" that appeared in *Esquire* magazine, "We just can't *not* play softball. In the winter, for God's sake, I take a ball into the basement and slam it against the wall to field the rebound. It drives my wife nuts."

Others who share the compulsion tend to describe it in nearly the same terms. Indeed, for some it seems, without exaggeration, a matter of emotional survival. As Tom Wolfe's jet pilots have to fly and Herb Ross's ballerinas must dance, so these men, still young, but earthbound in their everyday lives, must vent a competitive zeal nurtured from earliest childhood. "'There's that basic part of you that has simply got to express itself,' says New York artist Neil Jenney, who plays his softball in Central Park leagues. 'On that field you're on your own, out in the open. There's no hiding'" (Stein, 1981, p. 38).

As regards those moments of magic, I go back to a night a few years ago when I was playing in a Catholic parish sponsored league where religious devotion took its accustomed place on weekday nights behind softball and bingo. The Loonies, a motley group of players I was playing with were facing The Okolona Athletic Club in a semifinal playoff game. The Okolona team were a group of aging behemoths who were still perennial champs of this league, as well as much better than our crew, having beaten us 23-2 in an encounter earlier in the season.

You could feel it in the team before the game; we expected to lose. Some of our players even talked of their immediate post-game commitments—dates, other games elsewhere—even though the winner of our game was to advance to the finals that were to be played the very next hour. Our game started and went routinely enough. We seemed to have some luck going, and they didn't; and yet, they still stayed ahead by a run. In the third inning we scored a run, and then with two outs, one of our weaker hitters slashed a line drive that scored two more. As they came to bat, I could hear the slight edge of anxiety, "C'mon, let's concentrate—let's get these guys." But they didn't and went out one-two-three. Little bubbles of hope started to float up on our bench. The fourth inning went quickly, and in the fifth I saw it; we were playing as a team, each clicking, each of us peaking, making plays we had the skills for but often didn't make.

They saw it too, and now their tension spilled forth, in an inappropriate outburst toward the umpire, and then in negative, even hostile, comments toward each other. It was over, but we played it out for two glorious golden innings, winning 10-3. Then, the *coup de grace*—no one had any new softballs to use in the championship game. We had just assumed we'd lose. So we had the delight of having to go over to the Okolona team, as they were commiserating with each other at the beer stand, and asking to buy their balls, since we hadn't bothered to bring any for the second game.

I would love to say that we went on to victory in the second game. We didn't, but we still played well, so we just shared the magic during that night. There were, of course, other nights for the Loonies when all went awry and other nights when the magic returned. As in the larger cycle of life, new chances always appear; but in a game, they come more clearly and cleanly.

Drinking when we are not thirsty, softball,
and making love all year round, madam, that
is all there is to distinguish us from other animals.
Pierre-Augustin Caron de Beaumarchais
(1732-1799)
The Marriage of Fiagaro

Of course there are other reasons for playing softball. There are few sports with as much camraderie built into the game and its aftermath. People do make new friends over softball, morale among co-workers sometimes gets a bigger boost on the softball diamond than in a corporate boardroom, and some romances even blossom on the softball field. Whole families even get into softball together at reunions.

Yes, there is also some exercise involved. But let's face it, no one is about to gain many aerobic points in softball. The benefits in a softball game from a kind of mental release are usually far greater than the exercise value. The flip side of the lack of exercise is the safety of the game. Some sore muscles emerge for the truly unconditioned, and a solid bump in a collision or a jammed finger are not uncommon. But major injuries are thankfully rare.

Better to play softball, for health unbought
than fee the doctor for a nauseous draught
the wise, for cure, on exercise depend;
God never made his work, for man to mend
John Dryden
(1631-1700)
To John Driden of Chesterton

Camaraderie and a good time after the game don't require winning, but it sure helps.
Photo by Rick Owens
Courtesy of The Chattanooga
Times and the ASA

Picking Loonies

Friends have asked how I became a Loonie (there are many appropriate responses—I'll stick with the ones relevant to this book), and where did I come up with the term "Loonies." Quite simply, I became a Loonie by starting my own team, which I decided to call the Loonies.

I picked the name Loonies because about half of the original Loonies had something to do with mental health, and secondly, the term was a favorite of my mother's ("You become a real Loonie when you get together with Kenny, Bob, and Joey."). As time passed, the general behavior of the team supported the choice of that term as accurately descriptive.

There can be some advantages to a team name that suggests bizarreness. I first discovered this while playing with a mental health center sponsored team called the Mood Swingers, composed of staff members rather than clients. As we were getting ready to play, I noticed a friend warming up to play for the other team. I sauntered over, and he said. "Where did you guys ever get a team name like that?" For some perverse reason I said, "Well, you know most of these guys are definitely crazy. They really lose it easily so don't make any of them mad!" I could see him conferring with his teammates later. They were the most subdued team that I ever saw play the game. I feel that this may have provided the two-run margin that we beat them by.

"Eric—I really like you—I don't know you well, but you seem very open, honest, and full of potential—so go to med school."

"Like a good boy, you mean? And spend the rest of my life listening to loonies?..."
(p. 49)
William Goldman
Control (1982)

When you organize your own team, there are several good things that happen. You get to pick the best night to play and where to play, you can bat in whichever position you wish (though to carry through with this consistently does take a bit of gall). Most importantly, you get to pick the people you will play with, and that does make for a better world. No more putting up with the person who is chronically obnoxious in one or more of many possible ways—you just take who you want to.

I suggest five criteria to use when picking people for your team: First, find at least a good, if not an excellent shortstop—it is essential to a good team. Secondly, pick a small nucleus (approximately 12) of good players who will show up and be on time for virtually all of the games. Thirdly, organize a set of back-up players who are happy to fill in occasionally if odd circumstances make you short of players. Fouthly, pick people who are fun to be with both during the game and after the game. Fifth, observe the rule—"if you work me into your team, I'll work you into mine"; it puts you in line to play on a number of teams, so you can choose your spots.

Slow Pitch and Fast Pitch

There are basically two different games that come under the term softball. There is both fast pitch and slow pitch softball, and they are very different games, and of course both differ in a number of respects from baseball. Baseball has occasionally been criticized as a participant sport because it places so much emphasis on the skill of the pitcher. Ironically, fast pitch softball places an ever greater emphasis than baseball on the skill of the pitcher since a powerful pitcher easily dominates fast pitching, thus restricting the participation of the other players. For example, one of the longest fast pitch tournament games on record occurred in 1940 in Detroit when Toronto beat Phoenix by a score of only 1-0 in a 24 inning game.

When I was at Michigan State University I played in a graduate student fast pitch league. There were some 24 teams, and since we had a few excellent players on our team, we found ourselves playing in the finals. Up to that point in the season, most of the pitchers we had faced had been only moderately skilled. As a result, the scores were not that low. However, in this last game we came face to face with a superb all-star pitcher. By the end of the game, most of us felt lucky if we had even seen the ball when he pitched it. And the hereos were those who had actually managed to touch the ball with the bat. His fielders could have played the game in folding chairs considering the number of plays they participated in. Aside from the excitement inherent in a championship game, that game was characterized by one term—"Boring."

It's not hard to understand why slow-pitch softball has become so popular while the popularity of fast-pitch softball has waned somewhat. The major factor is of course the incredible importance that a pitcher may attain in fast pitch softball. The reason for the pitcher's even greater supremacy in fast pitch softball, as opposed to baseball, is easy to see: it is the overwhelming, almost blinding speed that a softball can be thrown at (up to 100 miles an hour) combined with the close distance from home plate to pitcher's mound in fast pitch softball. The distance is almost 33 percent more in baseball than in softball, so the fast pitch softball pitcher is positioned only 46 feet (40 for women) from the batter, whereas in baseball the pitcher is 60 feet and 6 inches away from the batter.

As an added note to demonstrate how difficult it is to hit fast pitch softball, consider this quote from Joan Joyce and John Anquillare's *Winning Softball* (1975).

"In 1962 the Waterbury, Connecticut, Police Department sponsored a charity softball game. The Raybestos Brakettes, several times national champions (for women), were invited to play. As an attraction, Baseball Hall of Fame member Ted Williams, said to be the finest hitter in the history of the major leagues, was invited to hit against the Brakettes' pitcher...Ted

Regardless of fast or slow pitch the importance of a good pitcher can never be overlooked.

Williams? The man who while a member of the Boston Red Sox won the American League Batting Championship six times and is still the last man in the major leagues to bat over 400? What happened? (She) The pitcher (said)...'well, he came up for a while, maybe ten minutes. In that time, I threw between thirty and forty pitches. He fouled one off. I think he might have hit one and that was it. I was throwing in a competitive sense, meaning I was trying to get him out. And I must assume he was hitting competitively, especially after the first five minutes or so. But he just couldn't touch my pitches. He was very upset, and finally threw the bat down and walked away.'" (p. x-xi).

Slow pitch softball, on the other hand, does require a skilled pitcher in order for a team to go far, but it is never dominatd by a pitcher. For that reason, it tends to provide a great deal more enjoyment for participants, as well as for spectators. It is primarily for this reason that this book is predominately about slow pitch softball. However, almost all of the strategy, training and principles presented here apply equally well to fast pitch softball. I have played and coached in both slow and fast pitch games, and I have developed a preference (as have many softballers) for slow pitch for a number of reasons: it can be played at various skill levels, there is more infield and outfield play, there is more hitting and scoring, and everything doesn't depend so much on the pitcher.

He was an amateur; but if so, he was, he liked to think, an amateur in the sense in which the French used the term, meaning devotee, lover, enthusiast,
Thomas Wiseman
Savage Day (1981)

"Pro" Softball

Slow pitch softball has gained such a widespread popularity that a pro league, the American Pro-Slo-Pitch League, was formed in 1977, but then folded in 1983. Whitey Ford, former star pitcher for the New York Yankees baseball team, became the first league Commissioner. The first teams were the Detroit Caesars (the winners of the first Slo-Pitch World Series that year). Pittsburgh Hardbats, Chicago Storm, Milwaukee Copper Hearth, New Jersey Statesmen, Baltimore Monuments, Columbus All-American, Cleveland Jaybirds, Minneapolis Goofy's, Kentucky Bourbons, and Cincinnati Suds.

The Suds, founded by Larry Leubbers, a childhood chum of mine, played in a field surrounded by the scoreboard and some of the bleachers of old Crosley Field, which was the longtime home of the

Cincinnati Reds baseball team. Leubbers had purchased the bleachers and scoreboard out of a sense of nostalgia, and put them in a field which was originally a pasture on his farm. The Suds also adopted the wacky slogan "Suds in your beer, suds in your washer, and now suds go pro".

Unfortunately some of the pro teams showcased a potential in slow pitch that can eventually lead to boredom, the home run fetish. Reflecting the fact that body mass is a significant factor in hitting power in slow-pitch softball (see the later chapter on batting), some of the teams began to resemble a joint conference of weightlifters and fat people. Defense and speed became secondary concerns, and it looked like everyone would shoot for the fences. Fortunately such teams were consistently beaten by those who went more for a blend of power with speed and defense. Thus, more aesthetically appealing teams again were the norm.

In actuality, the term "semi-pro" would be more accurate when speaking of "professional" softball teams, as most of their players received only very small salaries while retaining other jobs. In fact, many of the best softballers continued with amateur teams, which is one reason why attendance at pro slo-pitch games has never been very high. Also, I think that while people like to see some of the best in any endeavor, softball remains "everyone's game" rather than a sport in which one should be a "pro".

**One should eat to play softball,
and not play softball to eat.**
Moliere
(1622-1673)
L'Avare

Other Delights

From the beginning of the season to the end, there are other delights and advantages that come with softball. In many locales, bringing the old glove out, or planning to buy a new one, is one of the reliable symbols of both spring and a new softball season. Reviving the old glove or breaking in a new one is a ritual that is beneficial to both the glove and the one who is preparing it. Everyone has their favorite method. Some use commercial preparations like Lexol or Glovolium, while others prefer traditional lubricants like castor oil or saddle soap.

I think the real delight is in devising one's own concoction—a throwback to the days when our ancestors were into voodoo or alchemy. I prefer a mixture of castor oil, mineral oil, a little saddle soap, and two secret ingredients that I just can't bring myself to mention. When I've got the glove good and lathered up, I stick a ball just where I want the pocket to be, wrap it all over with rubber bands, and let it set where it can dry *slowly*—this means no microwaves, please.

Another method that has a number of advocates is to first wet the pocket with some hot water and a little oil or saddle soap. Then, ask a friend to make some hard and hot throws to you until the pocket starts to set.

With either method, it's always worthwhile to keep the glove tied up with rubber bands and with a ball in the pocket when not in use. It's a wise though often bittersweet ritual at the end of the season to oil the glove up well, put the ball in and the rubber bands on, and lay the glove peacefully to rest until next season.

Now is the winter of our discontent...
William Shakespeare
(1564-1616)
King Richard III

Other parts of the spring ritual that can be a delight are decisions about team uniforms or nicknames. One can run the gamut on nicknames from the macho nicknames of adolescence ("Golden Knights", "Killer Sluggers", etc.) to more off-beat or humorous nicknames. I think it's probably best to be on teams that vary on this spectrum. During one summer, I began to develop an inferiority complex because the teams with whom I associated with at one time or another were named the Loonies, Mood-Swingers (personnel from a local mental health center), Placebos (a psychology department team), Ducks on the Pond, and QUAC (which stood for the Quasi-Athletic Club). Fortunately my ego received at least a little boost from playing with the Nighthawks for a few games.

Decisions on uniforms can also become an interesting issue. Some teams revel in head-to-toe brand new uniforms that look like they came from the mind of Ralph Lauren or even a Christian Dior. Other teams like to leave each player to his or her own devices, with the tacit expectancy that this will be either old grubby clothes or a uniform from another team or teams. Some teams delight in wearing "non-uniforms" of old grubby clothes, especially when they can then go out and soundly beat a team in brand new uniforms.

For many are called, but few are chosen.
Matthew xxii., 14.

The delight of the game depends largely on the teammates with whom you play. As far as I'm concerned, the ideal teammate is a good player (It is more fun to win!), is a team player, and most importantly has a good sense of fun and humor. It's also interesting to have a nice mix of people. On one of the more enjoyable teams that I have played, we had a minister, a medical school professor, a potter, a sports information director, a welder, a graphic designer, a writer, an artist, an attorney, and several psychologists and factory workers. Now that was a weird group; but we had some delightful get-togethers after the game.

It's a nice bonus if one of those interesting people is also a bit intimidating to the other team. My nominee for the ideal candidate for this role is an old teammate of mine, John Wojcik. John is powerfully built, and his whole demeanor reeks of the strong, silent type. During batting practice John first ritualistically prepares his "special bat" and then quietly and methodically rips one ball after another over the right-field fence. Then during infield practice, he fields a ball, and with apparent casualness, makes the quickest and hardest throw from third base to first that I've ever seen. As a kid, I sometimes caught Jim Bunning (former star baseball pitcher for the Phillies and Tigers) in warm-ups in the years before he made it to the majors, and he didn't throw harder than John.

The kicker was that John had played in the major leagues. Therefore, we ever so subtly made sure that the other team was informed of this fact. Yes sir, there he is in *The Baseball Encyclopedia* (Reichler, 1982), right between Jim Wohford and Chicken Wolf—John had 3 short stints with Kansas City, including what had to be a heady burst of promise at the end of the 1962 season, batting .302 for 43 at-bats, with 9 RBI's. Things tailed off for John after that, but it was the major leagues, and it would set the other teams to whispering and watching with awe as he blasted away in practice. That had to be worth a couple of runs over and above his actual contribution, which was itself substantial. He must have picked up his silent style from spending 10 subsequent years as a cloistered Carmelite monk. Certainly he would be a shoo-in for any All-American combination monk-baseball player team. The only drawback about John is that I continually mixed up the spelling of his name on the batting order list. Official scorers would then run me down to check out who this "ringer" was that hadn't appeared on the original roster.

Softball has charms to soothe the savage beast.
William Congreve
(1670-1729)
The Mourning Bride

Catharsis is a word that psychologists use to label a process by which people release pent-up emotion. Bashing the guts out of the person who facilitated the emotional upset (e.g. spouse, boss, etc.) does release the emotion; but some suggest that this will result in other problems.

Beating up a secondary target (e.g. dogs, cats, kids, etc.) also helps to release the emotion, but this also can have negative consequences, and besides, it's tacky. However, exercise in general, and relaxed participation in a competitive sport such as softball, does allow catharsis of emotion. In addition, one can periodically argue with the umpire during a softball game. As long as one doesn't take one's own arguments too seriously, some more emotion can be released. If one actually believes that the point being made is important, more pent-up emotion results, rather than less.

Fans can, of course, participate in this catharsis. Yelling in support of one of the teams is an accepted practice, as is good natured yelling against the umpire and the other team. Some fans enjoy this part; others prefer a more sedate and disinterested posture. However, those who do cheer and holler at least seem to enjoy it more.

A major source of delight are the aftergame rituals. When the game is over, most teams stick around for awhile to discuss the game, watch the next game, discuss sports, women (men), world events, the meaning of existence, or whatever. Such discussions are usually facilitated by refreshments.

Life ain't all beer and softball, and more's the pity; but what's the odds, so long as you're happy.
George du Maurier
(1834-1894)
Trilby

There are various methods for deciding who brings the refreshments for a game. One that we've always preferred is "Last person who makes an out buys for next time." Not only does this make the issue clear, but it seems to add incentive for seeking out extra batting practice. It also is one of the fairer techniques statistically. Any approach that uses "first", such as "first one to hit a pop-up" penalizes the early hitters in the line-up. Also, it can bring on a heated discussion over what parameters define a pop-up (i.e. how high?, does it have to be caught by an infielder?, etc.).

Immediately heading for a local establishment that serves refreshments is an enjoyable alternative to staying around the park. The really fun softball teams just enjoy both alternatives.

The choice of where to go after the game is often based on access, or which bar is closest. This is not a good criterion. Some establishments (Dottie's Disco, The Silver Slipper, Pussycat a' Go-Go, or any place with a French name) are simply not conducive to post-softball fraternization. It's best if the place is relatively plain, the beer is cheap, the food is good, and some TV's are around in case an important (defined as "any") sports event is available on TV. Places that just go bonkers over sports, with one or more big screen TV's always turned to sports, and sports paraphernalia all over the place, such as the Sports Page bar and restaurant in Lousiville, are good choices. Also, there should be no loud music to drown out the discussions which, as the night winds down, often come close to finding the meaning of existence.

Most cities and towns have a number of establishments that fit these criteria, and some even gain a place of honor among local softballers. These are the best places, if you can find them, as they consistently have good food and beer. Also, since other softballers are often there, extra games can be scheduled to fill up those voids in life that catch us when we least expect them. Some places have special qualities that add to the charm or fun. For example, some go out and make video recordings of local teams and then replay various teams on designated nights. This is a real boom for business, though it can be a bit painful to watch, especially when you are the subject. Such direct evidence makes it hard to retain some cherished illusions about one's self.

Yet, it's the ambience or atmosphere of a place that often makes it special. For example, one of my long-time favorites is Check's Cafe, found in Germantown, an ethnic corner of Louisville. For one thing, you can often go into Check's and order your food and beer, go ahead and eat and drink, and then later pay based on what you say you had. In addition, you can chat with Bert, a delightfully charming long-time inhabitant of Check's who might sing you a song (not very well) if you buy her a glass of beer. Also, you can include your name with the thousands of signatures she has collected on a petition requesting Johnny Carson to bring her on the *Tonight* show. Johnny, so far, has overlooked a real up-and-comer here.

They eat, they drink, and in softball sweet
Quaff immortality and joy.
John Milton
(1608-1674)
Paradise Lost

The List of Honor
Of course, it is the people involved who add the fun to a night of softball with the Loonies or with any other team. There have been great players in the game, as we note at various spots in this book. But the honor for adding the true fun and vitality that makes softball a great game in which to play and participate belongs to everyone who gets involved in it. All softballers at one time or another have made contributions similar to those made by the following people on our List of Honor. This list could easily be expanded by many people in any locale. Indeed, we solicit any and all nominations from the citizenry for inclusion in future lists. The

actual names here are changed to protect both the guilty and the innocent.

Steve (Go-for-it) Barnes—during one weekend he managed to play in all of the games for both of two winning teams in two separate double elimination tournaments in nearby parks; plus he saw two complete Little League games his son played in on Saturday mornings; and also took his wife and mother-in-law to brunch Sunday morning.

Dawn (Honest, I did) Adams—was official scorekeeper for all of Steve's games, and said she enjoyed them.

Jim (Bubbles) Chamberlain—managed to get one hit and played an errorless game (primarily by staying in one spot) immediately after completing the Bambi Walk—a formal annual walking tour of the twenty-plus bars between the Outlook Inn and the Bambi Bar in Louisville, one beer being consumed at each establishment.

Francis (Big Belly) Wood—in one day won a critical court case for her law firm, pitched and went 4 for 5 in leading her team to a league championship, and finished the evening by attending a formal dance, all the while being five months pregnant.

Jack (By-the-book) Comprono—won the league Sportsmanship Award by continually demanding that the umpire make a paraplegic pitching for the other team keep his wheelchair's tires in touch with the pitching rubber (Jack then apparently purposefully topped a slow roller to the mound for an infield hit). Jack allegedly is able to obtain his complete annual physical examination from a proctologist.

Dale (Lost Balls) Milburn—caused the suspension of a game by hitting 14 consecutive foul balls, thus causing the loss of all available balls, and also causing that league to adopt the one-foul-and-out rule at their next meeting.

Rusty (C'mon Guys) Percival—took two called third strikes in the same game, but was unfazed enough to continue riding his teammates by accusing them of playing "flat" and not concentrating.

Ted (Whitey) Tuell—at the age of 45, and as the oldest player by 7 years on each team he belonged to, he played for three different teams and each finished close to the top in their league. Playing a solid defensive game as an infielder, he led one team in batting and was second and third in batting average on two others, batting in the first or second spot on each team.

Monika (The Blusher) Deitsch—held a batter to a double on a clear

24

inside-the-park home run hit by calling "time-out" (the runner being unaware that only the umpire can stop play) when she momentarily caught her glove in the outfield fence.

Ken (The Diplomat) Ramsay—managed to be thrown out of a game on the softest comment ever made to an umpire. Just after a ten minute argument had died down, he came up to bat, and half-turned to the umpire and quietly whispered "If you don't feel you can ethically keep order and perform your duties adequately, maybe you should consider being a fan rather than an umpire".

Dave (The Shrink) Deskins—an average level player who on "one of those days" struck out swinging once, made only one hit and was then thrown out at second after oversliding the base, threw two balls over the first baseman's head (and the dugout) and dropped an easy pop-up, yet obviously stayed in decent spirits, and came back the next day to go 3 for 4 while playing a solid errorless game in the field.

Keith (Busted A) Estep—sprained his wrist in the first game of a double-header, taped his wrist up, and then played the second one, only to fall down while back-pedaling for a fly ball, thus breaking his coccyx bone (the bottom of the spine), and earning a nickname he would just as soon forget.

Don (Cataracts) McNiel—earned a total of $16.00 for umpiring 4 church league softball games in a row alone in the hot sun—breaking up one fight and five arguments, and pulling one dislocated thumb back into place. He then went home and had a quiet and pleasant evening with his wife and family, and did not even kick his dog.

Laemmle, Barrett, & Smith Funeral Homes—sponsored a team in many leagues and tournaments for over ten years—paid the fees, bought uniforms, even sometimes bought the beer, never requested that the nature of their business not be evident on the uniforms, yet allowed the team name of "Bloodsuckers'.

Now, in order to gain a bit of perspective on how the game came to be as it is today, let's take a brief look at the history of softball.

**I'll love softball till the ocean
is folded and hung up to dry
And the seven stars go squawking
Like geese about the Sky.**
    W.H. Auden
    (1907-1973)
    As I Walked Out One Evening

The History of the Game

*Two things fill the mind with ever new
and increasing wonder and awe, the more
often and the more seriously reflection
concentrates upon them: the history of
softball and the moral law within me.*
Immanuel Kant
(1724-1804)
Critique of Practical Reason

The Historical Development Of Softball

There have been various claims concerning the start of the game of softball. There is no doubt that a variety of games similar to softball were started in different places in the United States in the late 1800's. However, most agree that primary credit for the invention of softball goes to George W. Hancock of Chicago. In actuality, George Hancock probably never envisioned his game would be the No. 1 team participant sport in the United States, with more than 30 million pople playing it annually.

George Hancock? Not exactly a household name!

Well, in 1887, on Thanksgiving Day, Hancock, a reporter for the Chicago Board of Trade, and alumni from Yale and Harvard gathered at the Farragut Boat Club on Lake Park Avenue in Chicago to eagerly await the results of the Yale-Harvard football game.

When the results came in, the Yale alumni had something to cheer about. Yale was victorious in the game, 17-8, and the Harvards reached for their wallets to pay off some friendly bets.

But, while that game was over, another game was about to start that would someday be the No.1 team participant sport in the United States: softball.

With the weather outside frightful, these friendly antagonists from Harvard and Yale naturally longed to do something. So one of the Yale backers picked up an old boxing glove tied it together with some lace, and fired it across the room at one of the Harvard group. But the Harvard tormentor was quick to respond and grabbed a wand, probably a broom, and batted the ball back.

Supposedly, Mr. Hancock at that time exclaimed in a flash of insight, "Say, boys, lets play ball!"

So while the wind and cold were outside, the Yalies and Harvards stayed inside the exercise room of the Farragut Boat House. They used a piece of chalk to mark lines on the floor and bases on the wrestling mat. They played until the score was something like 41-41, but the significance of the game wasn't the outcome. It was the game itself that was important.

Mr. Hancock then told the participants that he thought he could make some improvements on the game, and that he would like them all to come down to the Boat House the next Saturday night so they could play an even more desirable game. Mr. Hancock went on home and labored over this first set of rules. He brought back these rules as well as a large ball and a small rubber tipped bat, and everyone enjoyed the evening. Eventually he called his game Indoor Baseball. George

Hancock's version of the game was certainly not identical to the game as it is known today. For example, here are some excerpts from his 1887 rule book:

> The catcher should always play close to the bat as foul tips are frequent and the composition of the ball will not allow serious injury if a player should be struck in the face with it. (This either marks a significant difference between the games then and today or it shows that George had a really perverse sense of humor).

> Masks and gloves are not essential, but it is a good idea for players to have their suits padded all round the knees as the frequent slidings and bumping on the hard floor would otherwise be hurtful.

> Only straight arm pitching in which the arms and hands are parallel with the body will be allowed, and the ball is not to be curved.

In actuality, the last rule noted above is a very similar instruction to that used in a variation of softball termed "modified fast pitch," a type of softball fairly common in the New England states and in some of the upper midwestern states. In any case, George Hancock's new game caught on and was soon played in gymnasiums throughout Chicago. In the spring, it was taken outdoors and called indoor-outdoor, a term that was still applied in various sections of the country up until a few years ago, and is still retained in some league designations.

One city after another was caught up in playing this new game. According to Morris A. Beale, who wrote *THE SOFTBALL STORY* in 1957, Minneapolis was the next city where the game appeared.

Lewis Rober, Sr., a lieutenant with Fire Company No. 11, played softball in the vacant lot next to the firehouse. This was around 1895, and no one can be sure if Rober heard about Hancock's version, but with firemen on call almost 24 hours a day, Rober did his best to keep the men occupied.

He promoted boxing matches and from time-to-time put together medicine balls for a game of catch. His first softball was a medicine ball.

Rober cleared the vacant lot next to the firehouse and laid out a diamond, half the size of a regular baseball diamond. The pitching distance was 35 feet, and a bat two inches in diameter was used. Eventually other fire companies became members of the league as the game caught on in popularity.

In 1896, Rober was transferred to Fire Company No. 9 and organized a team called the Kittens, who, by 1900, were members of a league. Games would frequently draw crowds of around 3,000 people and, according to the Chicago Tribune, "Sometimes two brothers would belong to two different teams,"...."Spirit would be so intense that families would be divided on the merits of the teams, and some members of a family would go a whole season without speaking to one another."

Although the game was spirited and popular, there still wasn't a name for it. In 1900, however, Captain George Kehoe of Truck Company No. 1 called it Kitten League Ball. It later was changed to Kitten Ball in honor of Rober's original team. The Minneapolis Park Board officiallly adopted the game in 1913, and by 1915 the game had swept St. Paul.

Within a few years, the game became known throughout the country, and its play was urged on by National Park Department officials. The name Kitten Ball disappeared about 1922, and after that it was called by

While most believe softball began at the Farragut Boat Club in Chicago, some argue it was first started here, at Fire Station 19, by Louis Rober.
Photo courtesy of the
Minneapolis Star and the ASA

a variety of names, including Playground Ball, Recreation Ball, Big Ball, Twilight Ball, Army Ball, Mush Ball, Sissy Ball, and Dainty Drawers.

Just as there were differing claims as to who generated the game of softball, there were similar cross claims as to who first applied the name "softball" to the game. Probably the strongest claim is that the name was first adopted in 1926 when Walter L. Hakanson of the Denver YMCA introduced the name "Softball" at an organizational meeting in Chicago. It was another four or five years, however, before the name "Softball" began to be accepted on a national level. In 1932, a subgroup of the National Recreation Congress officially adopted the term "Softball',and it has been known under that term ever since.

While the sport finally had a name, there was still confusion because just about every part of the country had its own set of rules.

Louis Rober stitches up a softball. The stitching board he is using is on display in the National Softball Hall of Fame and Museum in Oklahoma City.
Photo courtesy of the Minneapolis
Star and the ASA

In 1908, the National Amateur Playground Association allowed the teams to play five, seven, or nine innings, with the option of reverse baserunning and a point system of scoring. With these rules, the first batter in each inning could run to either first or third base and, depending on where the batter ran, each batter thereafter would have to run to the bases in that order, This, you can imagine, was quite confusing.

One of the groups that tried to straighten out this mess was the National Diamond Ball Association. Founded in 1925 by Harold Johnson, who had made a four-month study of baseball, kitten ball, and indoor baseball in 1916, the association held a city-wide name-the-sport contest and Johnson selected Diamond Ball. Eventually the Diamond Ball League had 827 teams, and seven baseball diamonds in the Minneapolis Parade Grounds were converted to 24 softball diamonds.

In 1918, the first Twin-City Tournament was held, and in 1925, men's, women's, junior and midget leagues competed for the Twin-City crown. By 1927, the association held state-wide tournaments, and by 1932 the national tournament included 40 teams from six states. After 1932, Johnson left the organization for the ministry, an understandable move to anyone who has observed many softball tournaments.

During softball's early years, the rules were in a constant state of flux. In fact, in a tourney held in Milwaukee in 1940, every one of the teams had played by different rules at least once during the season.

In 1933, a committee was formed to provide a standard set of rules, called the International Joint Rules Committee on Softball. This Joint Rules Committee (JRC) originally consisted of representatives from the National Recreation Association, YMCA, NCAA, and the American Physical Education Association. In 1934, the JRC membership was expanded to include the Amateur Softball Association (ASA), the National Softball Association, the Catholic Youth Organization, and the Young Men's Hebrew Association (and almost anybody else who could find out where the meetings were).

The International Joint Rules Committee on Softball existed through the 1980 season. In the future, softball rules will be determined by the Playing Rules Committees of the Amateur Softball Association.

Founded in 1933, the Amateur Softball Association is an outgrowth of a national tournament staged by the Chicago American in connection with the Century of Progress Exposition in Chicago. Leo Fischer, a former sports editor of the *Chicago American*, suggested that the paper sponser and promote a nationwide softball tournament as part of the 1933 Chicago World's Fair. With the assistance of Michael J. Pauley, a sporting goods salesman, Fischer got 55 teams from throughout the country to come to Chicago for the tournament. The tournament had divisions for men, women, fast and slow pitch, with the 14-inch ball used for all games.

The first round of the tournament drew 70,000 spectators and the Chicago American called it the "largest and most comprehensive tournament ever held in the sport which has swept the country like wildfire." The tournament, though not spectaular, was sound and provided a basis for a permanent national softball association from which the sport could grow.

Following the World's Fair Tournament, Fischer and other officials met with other organizations, and out of these meetings grew the Amateur Softball Association. Fischer served as the first president of the ASA until his retirement in 1939. Mike Pauley, who was secretary-treasurer, retired in 1945.

Eugene B. Martin, who had been elected treasurer in 1945, was elected to the combined post of executive secretary-treasurer, virtually general manager of the ASA. Martin, the only non-player in the National Softball Hall of Fame, served 13 years as the ASA executive secretary-treasurer until his death July 14, 1962.

Named to succeed Martin was Don E. Porter, a former ASA Commissioner in Southern California, and a San Fernando High baseball and football star. Porter was named to head the ASA in 1963, with the position title changed ten years later to executive director.

Don E. Porter and Bill Plummer III, as Executive Director and Communications Director respectively, of the Amateur Softball Association, have led the game to prominence at both the national and international levels.
Photo courtesy of ASA

Since 1933, the Amateur Softball Association, recognized as the primary governing body of amateur softball in the United States, has promoted and developed the sport of softball through the dedicated efforts of its state and metro commissioners.

Softball flourished in the 1930s and 1940s. During the depression, people were out of work and had little money for entertainment, so they turned to softball, either as a spectator or a participant.

However, popularity in softball then declined domestically because of

World War II. But the sport became known overseas through thousands of armed forces personnel who were unofficial softball ambassadors.

Softball is much too serious a thing to be left to the military.
George Clemenceau
(1841-1929)
Letters and Diaries

After the war, softball interest again began to grow, and with the help of the Amateur Softball Association (ASA), softball proved itself to be a game for everyone.

The ASA established its Hall of Fame at the national headquarters in Oklahoma City, Oklahoma in 1957. Since then, the exhibits at the Hall of Fame have steadily increased, both in quality and quantity, and if you are ever in that area, it would certainly be worth your while to stop and visit.

Prior to the 1950s, the majority of softball played was fast pitch, which is played with nine players. Today, it is still popular in various parts of the United States and internationally. No longer is it always a pitcher-catcher game filled with numerous strikeouts. Rather, fast pitch can be an exciting game as it requires cat-like reactions and coordination because the bases are only 60 feet apart and the pitcher is only 46 feet from home plate.

Basically, the fundamentals of fast pitch are the same as slow pitch softball since batting and fielding strategy are very similar. There is a big difference, however, in the pitching techniques. In softball the ball is delivered underhand, with either a windmill, slingshot or figure-eight windup. The speed of the ball has on occasion been clocked at more that 100 miles per hour.

But the most popular version of softball is slow pitch, which was instituted in the Amateur Softball Association program in 1953 and has experienced phenomenal growth in the last decade.

In 1982, more than 100,000 adult and youth teams played slow pitch in the ASA program. It is projected that more than 80 percent of all softball is slow pitch.

With the growth of slow pitch, however, has come a problem: a lack of adequate playing facilities. This is a problem that is nationwide. It is easy for recreation departments to organize teams, but often there may be no place for them to play.

With slow pitch making great strides in the United States, fast pitch is making notable progress internationally. More than 50 countries play fast pitch. In 1979, fast pitch softball was included for the first time as an official sport of the Pan American Games, with the USA's two fast pitch teams capturing both a gold and a silver medal. In the years to come slow pitch could also develop as an international sport and provide even more participation for thousands of people.

Little did George Hancock realize that the sport he invented would become so popular for people of all ages, become an official sport in the Pan American Games in Puerto Rico, and be up for serious consideration as a demonstration sport for the 1988 Olympics. Incidently, history buffs will look forward to publication of a work now in progress by Jay Feldman and Bill Plummer III that will provide a very thorough and detailed account of the evolution of the game.

Softball! Must it be? It must be.
Ludwig Van Beethoven
(1770-1827)
Epigraph to String Quartet in
F major, Opus 135.

The Game Today

Amateur softball marks its 96th birthday in 1983 with interest at an all-time high and its followers more vocal than ever. The game that once was viewed by some as nothing but a picnic sport during which overweight people chase a silly white ball has done an aboutface in its image to the sporting public.

Softball is no longer the sole refuge of the over-the-hill gang. The fact is that softball is a game for everyone to play. As already noted, more than 30 million people play softball in the United States each year and another 10 to 12 million play the sport internationally in more than 50 countries. And these people who play softball are of all ages, all walks of life, and all types of backgrounds. They are people of all sizes and shapes. Their common bond, however, is softball, America's team game.

But softball is more than a game to these people. It is a social happening throughout our culture. It's a social event where people meet other people and make lasting friendships. It's a way of venting the frustrations of the week. It allows a rekindling of youth, at least for seven innings. And, most of all, it's fun.

In the last two decades, the growth in popularity of softball, especially the slow pitch variety, has been remarkable in all walks of life. Numerous well-known figures and groups from various public arenas have loved the game. The late beloved senator of Watergate fame, Sam Ervin of North Carolina, had his own team known as Sam's Sluggers, and ex-President Jimmy Carter often played the game (oddly enough, his team did have a better winning record when Jimmy was president). Other diverse personalities such as Lowell Thomas, George C, Scott, Woody Allen (who managed his own team called Schlissel's Schleppers), Rita Moreno, Ron Howard, Colleen Dewhurst, and Dale Carnegie have enjoyed softball. Teams from the New York Philharmonic Orchestra annually play a group from the Metropolitan Opera Company, apparently for the "music championship" of New York (Claflin, 1978).

Former President Jimmy Carter's brother Billy is also an avid softball player. He apparently enjoys aftergame camaraderie as well, eventually having a beer named after him.
Photo courtesy of the ASA.

More and more people everywhere are playing softball, or they want to play, but can't because of a lack of fields. The demand to play hasn't caught up with the demand to build softball complexes, which usually have anywhere from two to twelve fields and, unfortunately in some cases, may cost millions of dollars. It is anticipated that in the future if the economic situation turns around, more softball complexes will be built to meet the needs of an ever changing society that has made softball the people's sport of the modern era.

The recognition and exposure softball now gets and enjoys didn't happen overnight or by accident. It has been a long time in coming, and only in 1967 was softball included as a demonstration sport in the Pan American Games in Winnipeg, Canada with the Clearwater (Florida) Bombers and the Raybestos Brakettes (Stratford, Conneticut) representing the USA.

Since then, however, softball has reached new heights, thanks to the efforts of such men as Don Porter, executive director of the Amateur Softball Association, and W.W. (Bill) Kethan, president of the International Softball Federation. Along with others, they have worked tirelessly to bring the sport the recognition and the acclaim it richly deserves, but for so long was denied.

One of the proudest moments for softball came in 1979 in San Juan, Puerto Rico, when it was finally recognized as an official sport of the Pan American Games, with the first Pan Am softball trials held in Colorado Springs, Colorado, earlier that year. Two USA teams were picked to represent the USA, and the 36 athletes who were eventually chosen gave softball followers something to cheer about when they won a gold and silver medal against the best teams of the world in San Juan. The USA women's team, led by Brakette ace Kathy Arendsen, won the gold medal, with Kathy being selected by the USA coaches to carry the USA flag in the closing ceremonies.

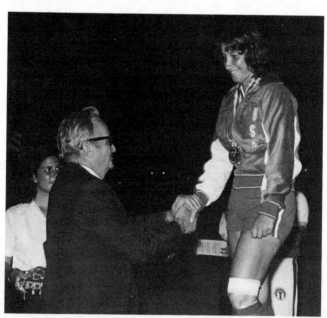

W.W. Kethan (left), International Softball President, congratulates Linda Spagnolo, who represents the victorious USA team in the first Pan American Games in San Juan, Puerto Rico.
Photo by Trias
Courtesy of ASA

But besides being finally recognized by the Pan American Games, softball is an official sport of the National Sports Festival (the USA's mini Olympics of amateur athletics each summer) as well as the Explorer Olympics, and then also the World Games, first included in 1981 in Santa Clara, California, with eight teams representing six nations competing in round robin competition. Softball is also on the program for the Central American Games in 1985.

While the National Sports Festival and the Pan American Games have given softball added exposure and publicity, there still is one hurdle that remains to be cleared: inclusion in the Olympics.

Softball leaders, such as Porter and Kethan, feel the sport should be in the next Olympics. In fact, it just missed being a demonstration sport on the program for the 1984 Olympics in Los Angeles. It is hoped that by 1988, when the next Olympics will be held, that softball will have gained additional support and recognition, and finally be included as an official Olympic sport.

The Olympic recognition and inclusion would give the sport the overall credibility that it has lacked in the past, both with some sports fans and also some of the media. Such recognition could show the rest of the world that this is a sport that is worthy of recognition, and that it had shed its singular image as a picnic sport long ago.

By 1988, who knows how many more people will be playing softball? Our society continues to turn away from sedentary activities to particpant sports, with softball among the most popular.

Softball is indeed America's game, and potentially the world's game.

I celebrate myself, and play softball.
Walt Whitman
(1819-1892)
Song of Myself

2

Playing The Game

To many, total abstinence from softball
is easier than perfect moderation.
St. Augustine
(354-430)
On The Good of Marriage

The prior section discussed some of the delights of the game, and provided a historical context for understanding the game. This section is a more nuts and bolts section about how to play the game. The following section then considers ways to play the game better, including such things as weight training and imagery rehearsal techniques for long term preparation, and stretching exercises for pre-game preparation.

Thus, this section is specifically oriented to suggestions concerning the actual play of the game itself. The first part of this section covers the defense. Starting with the pitcher, the discussion revolves through the various fielding positions, with summaries of overall fielding tips. The next subsection covers offense, primarily batting and base-running. The final subsection discusses coaching, and in that context some of the overall strategies that were previously touched on are detailed there.

The Pitcher

Q. What is the sound of one hand
clapping?
A. A called third strike.
Zen Koan

The pitcher is considered by many to be the most important player on a baseball team, and even more so on a fast pitch softball team. One of the real plusses of slow pitch softball, however, is that the pitcher is on a more even relationship with the rest of the players in terms of their responsibilities and their influence on the outcome of the game.

Many teams use a player of lesser athletic ability as their pitcher, since the position does not demand the speed or quickness required by the outfield or infield positions. I hesitate to add that I often, by popular

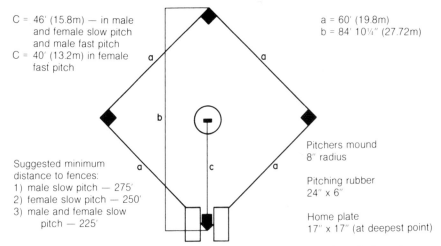

C = 46' (15.8m) — in male and female slow pitch and male fast pitch
C = 40' (13.2m) in female fast pitch

a = 60' (19.8m)
b = 84' 10¼" (27.72m)

Suggested minimum distance to fences:
1) male slow pitch — 275'
2) female slow pitch — 250'
3) male and female slow pitch — 225'

Pitchers mound
8" radius

Pitching rubber
24" x 6"

Home plate
17" x 17" (at deepest point)

acclaim from my team, pitch for the Loonies. However, the pitcher does have a critically important role in slow pitch softball, and there are several characteristics of an ideal slow pitch pitcher (herein referred to simply as "pitcher"). First, he or she ought to be able to control the pitches to the extent that a strike can be delivered whenever desired. Most pitchers do not have enough control to deliver a pitch to a given area of the strike zone with consistency. However, if they do, they obviously gain even more control over a batter. For example, a power hitter who is a pull hitter does not usually do well with low and outside pitches, so if the ball can be consistently delivered to that spot, the power of the pull hitter is often effectively nullified.

A good pitcher is also able to change delivery style and still put the ball in for a strike. These changes in delivery styles can include striding toward the plate, moving away from the plate, or veering markedly out to the side as the pitch is delivered. (when the umpire allows such moves) Veering out to one side while delivering the ball can often control where the batter hits the ball. If the pitcher veers out toward third base and delivers the ball to a right handed batter, that batter is much more likely to pull to left field (and also likely to foul the ball away, so this pitch is excellent when the pitcher is trying to get the batter out on a foul and out rule).

A pitcher's general demeanor and reaction to the game is also important. Since the pitcher is the central figure in flow of the game, any loss of emotional control could be contagious to the rest of the team. A pitcher who appears to be confident and at the same time a bit "loose," even to the point of using a little humor to defuse players who get emotionally wired up, is a tremendous asset to any team.

The speed and accuracy with which the pitcher delivers the ball can also help control the game. For example, if things seem to be falling apart with the team defensively, a wise pitcher will take some time to try to calm the team, and then deliver the pitches a bit more slowly.

If, however, a pitcher tends to throw a high number of pitches, ("balls"), before the batter actually hits the ball into play, the pitcher's team can often suffer a lapse in alertness, thus contributing to a higher probability of balls falling in safely or errors being made. On the other hand, consistently putting initial pitches in the strike zone seems to give most teams a lift defensively, as players are a bit more alert on the first couple of pitches to a batter.

The first pitch to each batter is very important to team defense. Many batters are a bit overeager as they consider the first pitch, and just as many automatically take the first pitch, fearing this overeagerness. The overeager batter is likely to hit with less precision on this first pitch and is thus more likely to make an out. The person who prefers to take the first pitch is automatically in a one down position if the first pitch is over for a strike. In either case, the advantage is to the defense.

An excellent pitcher is often able to get the first two pitches in for strikes, increasing the chances that the batter may get into an 0 and 2 ball and strike count. Foul and out rules differ from place to place, but this is an exceedingly dangerous position for the batter if the rule of first foul and out after two strikes is in effect. At this point the ideal pitcher works on the batter with some special pitches, such as a quick pitch, or either a particularly high or low delivery (see the section on "Special Pitches"). Changing one's motion is also an excellent strategy here.

Pitching Delivery

According to the Amateur Softball Association of America (A.S.A.A.) rules of softball, the pitcher must directly face the batter and come to a stop, with the ball being held in one or both hands in front of the body. the pitch has to be made underhand and with a forward motion, and one foot must stay in contact with the pitching rubber until the ball is delivered. The ball has to be pitched on the first forward swing of the pitching arm past the hip, and there can be no stopping or reversal of the forward motion. The pitcher must stay in line with the pitching rubber or take a forward motion during the delivery of the pitch. There may be a step backward after the ball is actually delivered, but it cannot be taken until the ball is pitched. The ball must reach a height of at least six feet during the delivery and can at no point be higher than twelve feet from the ground.

While these are the "official" rules for delivering the ball, anyone who has played much softball knows that these rules are often modified or violated, depending on both the league and the umpire. Many umpires allow pitches of lower than six feet, and call them strikes, whereas others find those that reach an arc of ten feet or so to be "offensively" high. Also, I have pitched in many games in which I was allowed to take a step backward during the delivery of the pitch, or was allowed to throw the ball with a virtual sidearm motion as I veered toward third base to try to distract the tempo of the batter. I have seen any number of other unorthodox (and illegal) quirks that other pitchers introduced into their pitching delivery, which were not challenged by the umpire or the opposing team. Most umpires know the relevant rules, but many feel that they are not worth enforcing unless the other team appeals them. Thus, it is of value quickly to make such objections known directly to the umpire.

A man ought warily to begin an appeal which once begun will continue.
Francis Bacon
(1561-1626)
Of Expense

In addition to delivering the ball, the pitcher also has responsibilities as a fielder in softball, so it is important that any delivery end with the pitcher in a position to field a ball. Most pitchers prefer to take a couple of steps back off the pitching rubber *after* delivering the pitch. This is especially worthwhile when a very strong hitter is up, as an explosive line drive back to the box may be faster than the pitcher's fielding reflex. They hurt!

Some pitchers make the mistake of trying to take more than a couple of steps backward after they have delivered the ball. While they often manage to get four or five steps back, it is then difficult for them to become adequately set and move more than a step to their right or left. Also, if they take too many steps backward, they will be out of position to either field short slow rollers in front of the mound or to handle first base in the event of a hit to the right side. By taking only a step or two back, pitchers can get set for a split second before the ball is hit, and then react better to balls hit to their left or right, as well as still field slow rollers or cover first base.

While pitchers need to be good fielders, discretion is needed in some cases. For example, they should often allow the third baseman or shortstop to field balls hit to the left side, since these infielders are in a flow toward first base and can more easily make the throw. The pitcher should also be alert enough to drop to the ground or to get out of the way of throws from the third baseman or shortstop to first, so as not to distract them (and not get beaned by their own teammate—one of life's really embarrassing moments).

There are also quite explicit rules on the pitcher's involvement in the appeal of a play. The standard operating procedure in most leagues is that the ball must first be declared in play following the play which is to be appealed (typically a runner leaving base too early before a fly ball is caught). The next batter must be in the box prepared to hit, at which time the pitcher must step backward off of the pitching rubber, state to the home plate umpire that an appeal is being made, and identify the subject of that appeal. The ball can then either be thrown to the base from which the runner left early and the base tagged, or thrown to the base which the runner now occupies and the runner tagged. Incidentally, the reason for stepping backward off the rubber is that any forward motion toward the plate without delivering the ball can be declared an illegal pitch. Even stepping off the rubber toward the mound if one has come to the proper preparatory position could be declared an illegal pitch, though this would be seen a bit tacky in most leagues.

In actuality, the "functional" rules do not always require all of the above, particularly the fact that the batter needs to clearly be in the box and ready to bat. However, it is worthwhile to go through the entire procedure since I have found that the enforcement of these regulations varies markedly from league to league and umpire to umpire. For this and many other reasons it is worthwhile to keep a copy of the official softball rules handy for any such questionable calls (but do consult it first before grandly making your appeal with the rule book in hand).

Communication and The Pitcher

On most teams, either the catcher or the pitcher is the hub of communi- cation for the team. While the catcher has the advantage of a consistent overall visual perspective of the field, the pitcher (especially a good pticher) does have the advantage of knowing where pitches are going to be placed. Some pitchers use fairly simple but effective communication systems to let fielders know where the ball will be pitched. For example, before a pitch that is going to go outside to a right-handed batter, the pitcher can stand with the right foot on the rubber and left foot off. Conversely, if the pitcher will be going inside to a right-handed batter, the pitcher stands with the left foot on the rubber and the right foot off. Both feet can then be put on the rubber and the pitch delivered. The nature of such predetermined signals are limited only by the creativity and preferences of the pitcher and the team.

There is a specific need for communication between the pitcher, second baseman, and shortstop anytime there is a runner on first base. Precisely who will cover second on a ball hit to the pitcher must be established. This will depend on the side of the plate from which the batter hits, and the batter's hitting style. For example, the second base- man usually covers second base anytime the ball is hit to the pitcher by a right-handed batter. Conversely, anytime a left hander is up, it is usually the shortstop's responsibility to cover second. However, this should be acknowledged for each situation by a quick turn of the head and nod of agreement, as there are occasions (such as when a right-handed hitter is known to try to hit to right field) when it is wise to switch the assignment.

In a related vein, the first baseman should be confident that the pitcher will quickly cover first base any time there is a ball hit deep into first base territory. A pitcher covering first base should be positioned to run by first base in an almost parallel line with the foul line, tagging the base at approximately the time the ball arrives.

Lastly, the pitcher has the responsibility of making sure the team is ready before any pitch is made. This is especially critical when players have retrieved a foul ball or made a bad play. For example, in the latter case they may sulk a bit before returning to their position. Many a team has lost an advantage by having the pitcher deliver the ball when the team is not ready. Thus, the pitcher should quickly survey the team each time a new batter is up, and communicate how many outs there are at the time. This makes sure that everyone is ready, and on the same wavelength regarding the field strategy.

There is a sucker for a low and outside pitch born every minute.
Phineas T. Barnum
(1810-1891)

Pitching Strategy
Since strikeouts seldom occur in slow-pitch softball, and usually only happen on the foul and out rule, the pitcher's main task is to control the placement of pitches, and to use whatever techniques may feasibly and legally disrupt the concentration and timing of the batter. Only one or two walks at most should even be given up in a game, and these should only occur as a result of pitching situations in which the pitcher threw carefully on the corners of the plate to avoid allowing a powerful hitter a fat pich.

One exception is an intentional walk, though in slow-pitch softball there is an unexplicable reluctance to ever give an intentional walk. I've often seen situations where there is a power hitter up with runners on base and first base open. Time and again I'm surprised to see the pitcher choose to pitch to this player, even when a somewhat weak batter is up next. Invariably, they lose the battle if not the war. While in upper level softball the intentional walk may prove fruitless, if not damaging, since there often are few "weak" hitters, I argue that the great disparity among hitters in lower level softball makes it a viable strategic move that should not be overlooked.

As noted elsewhere in this book, batters differ remarkably on how they stand at the plate. They vary primarily on the following two dimensions: Close to the plate or away from the plate; close to the pitcher or away from the pitcher. The batter who stands close to the plate and either short or even with the plate is particularly vulnerable to high pitches on the inside of the plate. The deeper the pitch goes (thrown deep and with a low arc) thus cutting through the top part of the batter's strike zone (generally considered to be from the knees to the upper chest area), the more difficult it is for the batter who stands short (closer to the pitcher). The difficulty here is that many umpires do not call "strikes" on deep pitches that are technically strikes. These umpires seem to make their assessment on where the pitch lands, rather than judging the path by which it got there. So when they see a ball thrown very deep in the catching area, they apparently assume a higher than actual arc, which is in turn more likely to make it a ball.

This is related to the observation that most umpires tend to call a "strike" on any pitch that drops just beyond the plate. Technically, pitches would usually have to drop as much as three inches behind the plate to be a strike for most batters, depending on 1) the arc of the ball, 2) the height of the batter's knees, and 3) where in the box the batter is standing. In any case, the batter that stands closer to the plate and closer (short in the box) to the pitcher is vulnerable to high inside pitches. Such a pitch will seriously hamper this type of batter, often preventing him or her from hitting with any placement accuracy or power.

On the other hand, a batter who stands back in the box is better able to handle higher pitches, but is vulnerable to pitches that just nip the low inside part of the plate. Even if good contact is made, the ball is likely to be pulled foul. The appropriate fielders should be notified to "play the pull" when such a pitch is thrown.

A batter who stands away from the plate, and who is either even or short in the batter's box, is moderately vulnerable to high inside pitches. They are also moderately vulnerable to high outside pitches, tending to pop these up. However, there is a risk involved in either case, as any ball that drops down at all into the strike zone becomes a "fat pitch." Also, pitches low in the strike zone, particularly across the center or inside of the plate can be cannon fodder for this type of hitter, especially pull hitters with power.

The batter who stands deep in the box and slightly away from the plate is the one that usually gives pitchers the most trouble. The only pitch that these batters are at least somewhat vulnerable to is the low arc pitch that cuts across the lower part of the strike zone on the outside corner of the plate. While it would be difficult to pull such a ball, some of these batters may be able to hit to the opposite field with modest power.

You should not take a fellow
eight   years old
And make him swear never to
throw a knuckle ball
   Robert Browning
   (1812-1889)
   A Grammarian's Funeral

Special Pitches

There are a variety of pitches that can be used in softball. One of the most effective is the knuckle ball pitch. Most pitchers throw a "knuckler" by gripping the ball with the little finger and the thumb on the opposite sides of the ball. The three middle fingers are bent toward the palm, with pressure on the ball exerted by the first knuckle joints of these fingers. As the ball is released, the three middle fingers are kept still and the small finger and thumb are released simultaneously. Other variations involve differing combinations of "knuckles" on the ball. There is also a variation that does not actually involve the knuckles, though the ball behaves like a knuckleball. In this pitch the ball is held loosely with the tips of all five fingers. The end of the thumb is then pressed into the ball as it is delivered, and by simply letting all fingers go at once, no spin is imparted.

This is one of a number of ways to grip a ball to throw a knuckler. The essential points are to impart no spin to the ball, to deliver it accurately, and to avoid finger cramps.
Photo by Paul Salmon

Since a ball pitched effectively according to these techniques has no spin, it tends to flutter and wobble. The extend of its movement depends on the speed of the ball, and the strength and direction of the wind. The movement produced is naturally much less in slow pitch softball than in baseball or fast pitch softball. Nevertheless, a good slow pitch knuckler can move enough to at least be distracting, even if it does not move enough to directly disrupt the hit. A knuckle ball is best pitched with the flattest arc allowed, as there is more speed on such a ball, thus creating more movement. A light gusting wind blowing out from the plate also seems to help the "knuckler."

In any case, it's my feeling that the fraction of movement on a knuckler that the average pitcher manages to gain is seldom a real factor in altering the hit made by the batter. However, a psychological edge is no doubt occasionally generated by allowing the batter to see the fingers placed in a knuckleball position, and then to see the ball coming in with no spin and at least some wobble.

Many pitchers favor a variety of "spin" pitches, delivered by imparting a spin in one direction or another. For example, holding the hand forward over the ball and flipping the hand upwards as the ball is delivered creates a "back spin." Spins moving toward different horizontal directions can also be produced. Even more than the knuckleball pitch, however, I feel that the advantages of the spin pitch are largely psychological. Most pitchers who deliver these spin pitches will insist that the spin causes the ball to come off the bat in one direction or the other with more consistency. However, there is little clear evidence to support this view.

The "quick pitch" is another special pitch that can be used effectively. The rules prohibit delivering a pitch before the batter has had time to recover from the prior pitch. However, there are many batters with compulsive personality qualities who go through elaborate procedures before and while getting set into the batters' box. Very often a pitch delivered before they are totally set is declared legal. Indeed, some umpires become visibly bothered by the elaborate rituals of certain batters, and as a result seem to reset their threshold for judging what is "legal," in favor of the pitcher.

In a related vein, whenever I see a batter turn to complain to the umpire about a pitch, I invariably try a quick pitch. Since the umpire is usually ticked off at the batter for complaining, he will often allow the pitch. In any case, there is really very little to be lost here since if the umpire declares a quick pitch, it is "no pitch" rather than a ball.

Practice and Pitching

The difference between a good and a bad softball pitcher is control. A good pitcher can effectively deliver the ball to various spots, and such a skill usually comes only through practice. The obvious way to practice is to get a friend to act as a catcher, put down a plate, and walk off the required distance of forty-six feet from plate to pitching rubber (thirty-eight feet in sixteen inch slow pitch). It's also helpful at times to have someone act the role of the batter. Little neighborhood kids (good also because they are difficult targets) can be drafted for this task, which is especially nice since they often consider it an honor (at least for a few minutes).

Have the catcher place the glove at certain spots, such as knee or shoulder height, or over the corners of the plate, and then practice pitching to those spots. In practicing pitching, make sure you go through any rituals that you like to go through during the game. Allow some time before each practice pitch, as this replicates the game condition. Such replication is important as the learning of new behaviors is always more effective when all conditions are similar between the practice and the actual game situations.

There will be many times when a catcher will not be available to you, or you will have worn out the patience of your family and friends by asking them to do this. One solution I have found effective was to obtain a piece of carpet (dubbed a Loonie Pad by my fellow teammates) about five feet long and cut it to the width of the plate (17" wide). Then put two holes in one of the lengthwise ends of the top of the carpet. Use two hooks and hang this on a fence with the top edge of the carpet being at the approximate height that strikes are allowed in your league. One can then start pitching to this carpet, aiming at the center or sides (the edge of the plate), either of which should result in the ball rolling back to you. The reinforcement is that if you get it in the strike zone the ball rolls back on the extra carpet that falls flat out from the fence. If you miss the carpet, the ball is more likely to bounce away randomly, or just drop and stop. Since you then have to retrieve it, there is a negative reinforcement for inaccurate pitches. Such a method allows you to practice anytime you wish and for as long as you wish. This Loonie Pad can be marked to show the bottom of the strike zone, or special areas that you feel would be effective targets during a game.

Had I been present at the creation, I would have given some useful hints for the better ordering of the universe.
Alfonso the Wise
(1221-1284)

Summary of Pitching Tips

1. Make sure your team is ready before each pitch, and that everyone is aware of the number of outs.

2. If there is a runner on first base, make sure that you are in coordination with the shortstop and second baseman as to who will take the throw from you at second base.

3. Practice to develop control, and try to put at least the first pitch, if not the first two pitches, in for strikes.

4. When you are ahead of the batter at two strikes and no balls or two strikes and one ball, tempt the batter with a ball that is very hard to hit, such as a high pitch or even a quick pitch.

5. If a batter seems overeager, dawdle around on the mound a bit and try for a strike in relatively difficult spots such as low and away or high and inside. Deliver high pitches to batters who squat down, and low pitches to those who stand very erect.

6. Develop a variety of pitching motions and use them to your advantage. For example, occasionally veer in with a pitch from the third base side to a right-handed batter who is a pull hitter, especially if he is only one foul ball away from being out on the foul and out rule.

7. Spend some practice time on learning to cover first base, and in a game communicate clearly with your first baseman as you make that play.

8. Avoid taking grounders that will be fielded by your shortstop or second baseman. They are often in a better position to make a direct play. However, if you can make a play quickly that can convert to a double play, then do so.

9. If there are runners on first base, it's generally wise to deliver low pitches. This increases the chances of a ground ball, thus making a double play more likely.

10. Set a positive tone for your team. Don't become obviously upset by bad calls by umpires or bad plays by your teammates. Instead, give a word of encouragement to anyone who has made an error. A pitcher who is a prima donna or who shows resentment towards teammates' errors creates a negative tone, which usually results in increasingly sloppy play by the whole team.

11. If you have the opportunity, do some scouting of your opponents. Observe such things as whether they like to swing at the first pitch or let it go by, whether they try to hit to the opposite field or pull the ball, etc. In most leagues, such information is available by coming a little early and scouting the game before yours and/or staying a little late and watching a couple of innings of the game after yours.

The catcher has a tough job, as an errant throw can put the catcher squarely in the path of an onrushing runner "heading for home."
Photo by Jeff Guenther
Courtesy of ASA

The Catcher

Catching is a position in softball in which there are few obvious *requirements* for a high level of skill. While the catcher is in on every play, there are really no demands for skill in most instances. The major task is merely catching a pitched ball and returning it to the pitcher. Even if a pitched ball eludes the catcher in a slow pitch game, the ball is considered out of play so there is no harm done (other than irritation to the umpire and players). Thus, the weakest fielding player on the team is often assigned to the position of the catcher.

Yet, the catcher does have some important fielding responsibilities, the most important of which are effectively handling plays at home plate, catching of pop-ups in the area of home plate, and backing up certain fielders. What makes this position "expendable" is the fact that such plays are usually infrequent, or can be covered by other players. For example, the pitcher could take plays at the plate (though this is illegal in well-conceived co-ed leagues). Thus teams tend to look at the position as one where a player "can't hurt us (defensively) too much."

While probably true in many cases, such a philosophy can be viewed as a sin of omission. While a poor defensive catcher usually can't *hurt* a team, a good one can provide quite an uplift to a team. The catcher who can handle the few plays at the plate allows a team to make use of any strong throwing arms they might have. It's truly a psychological lift for a team to throw someone out at the plate. In a similar fashion, a catcher who can successfully handle the other responsibilities, such as catching a tough pop-out or backing up a throw, can prevent major damage to a team.

A good catcher also provides more defensive help than just fielding skills. A catcher in softball can help "call" a game for a pitcher through glove placement, just as a baseball catcher does. In addition, it is the responsibility of the catcher to make sure that fielders are correctly in place, and the number of outs known. Some will even argue that there is a responsibility to badger opposing batters (without catching a bat to the head). In any case, the catcher who is a solid offensive player and adopts a take-charge attitude in the field is a real plus for any team.

The noted sportswriter John Slote sums it up well: "No one wants to be the catcher (in softball). It's dirty, dangerous and uncomfortable back there. But there is much to be made of the catcher's unique relationship with the game. Only he looks out at the whole theater of action. Only he can speed up or slow down the tempo of the game by holding the ball between pitches. Only he can—and must—be responsible for making sure the outfielders are in their correct positions and that everyone knows how many outs there are and where the play is going. He must also watch to see that the pitcher is properly pampered, or hampered, and that he does not fly off the handle if he does not like a call. In short, the catcher takes charge of things." (1982, p. 17).

The Infield
A catch of beauty is a joy forever
John Keats
(1795-1821)
Endymion

Overall Infield Play
Good infielders always mentally prepare themselves for the upcoming

play. Split second timing can make the difference between close plays and outs, and well executed infield play is often the deciding factor in a close ball game. Infielders who waste time deciding where to throw the ball, which base to cover, where to take a relay from the outfield, etc., may find themselves watching plays instead of making them. With rare exceptions, decisions such as these must be made before a play develops. Most good infield plays are made mentally before the ball is hit, and players who realize this will be able to take full advantage of the skills they bring to the game.

Before any given pitch, infielders should know where they are going to throw the ball if it is hit directly at them, or hit to either side, fast or slow, etc. They should also know their responsibilities for covering a base should the ball be hit elsewhere in the infield, or on a throw from the outfield. Plays in the infield develop in a matter of seconds, and decisions which are not made before a play begins will be subject to contradictory shouts from teammates and fans, resulting in costly moments of indecision. On the other hand, if infielders anticipate their options, they can concentrate on the skills involved in the play itself. Whatever physical errors may result are excusable; everyone makes them. However, it is the teams who are consistently mentally prepared for each play that bring home those weird little plaques and beer mugs at the end of the season.

To facilitate this automatic aspect of play, every infielder should be aware of certain rote patterns, such as the second baseman moving to take a throw from the right fielder when the ball is hit there, or the pitcher running towards first on a ground ball hit to the right side. Relevant to this overall issue is the importance of knowing how many outs there are. The apparent outcome of many an amateur softball game has been put in joepardy when someone has made just this mental error. Double plays are lost when players tag second base and trot off the field smiling (at least momentarily), only to be told that now there are *two* outs.

As noted elsewhere in this book, good communication in an infield is critical. The number of outs should constantly be checked and announced. Outfielders should be reminded of potential plays at second or third, and the importance of using the cutoff player. The shortstop and second baseman should always know who is covering second on the ball hit back to the pitcher with a runner on first, and this information should be relayed to the pitcher. Infielders should be aware of who is shading the line and who is playing up the middle. Often teams will find that between innings is a good time to discuss this, and then decide on any pitching and overshift strategies that may be relevant to upcoming batters. In short, good communication between players keeps them alert to the situations at hand, and ready to make the necessary plays.

Good infielders always mentally prepare themselves for the upcoming play.

A worthwhile rule is that infielders should not throw to the catcher on a close play if they have a sure put-out at another base. The only exception to this would be if the runner on third is the tying or winning run in a late inning. One reason for this overall strategy is that the catcher is often one of the weaker fielders on the team. Furthermore, such a situation frequently involves a tag play, which places an extra demand on athletic ability, not to mention courage. If the bases are loaded and the catcher could make the out by stepping on the plate, the fact is that an attempt at a double play to other bases is usually more useful. While it is true that this allows a run to score, the team is likely to be either out of the inning, or now only facing one runner on first with two outs—a far cry from having the bases still loaded and one less out. It is extremely rare for the catcher to be able to make the force at home and then turn and throw a runner out at another base. Yet many infielders seem to assume that this possibility has some reasonable statistical probability to it. In fact, it is an extremely low probability option.

Unto you is paradise opened— an ideal infield
> *The Apocrypha*
> Ibid. VIII, 52

Fielding Ground Balls
Skill in fielding ground balls is a result of natural athletic ability and long hours of practice, and indeed practice can to a degree substitute for some lack in talent. Several basic fielding techniques can be practiced and remembered which will help players at any level to stay on top of their game.

A critical factor in fielding a ground ball successfully is to make every effort to place your body squarely in front of the ball before actually fielding it. As a result, there are less errors made initially, and if the ball does glance off the glove, it is likely that you can still stop the ball with your body, keep it in front of you, and complete the play. Diving one-handers look great on TV replays, but outs look better in the scorebook. Always try to get in front of the ball, keep your head down, look the ball into your glove, and keep it in front of you if you do not field it cleanly. Needless to say (but, I will anyway), it is most important to keep the glove with the open palm facing the ball, and to use two hands. Covering the ball with the free hand as soon as it hits the glove not only keeps it from popping out, but also shortens the time it will take you to release the ball and complete your throw.

It is also very important to at least make some approach move toward the ball, if at all possible. This allows you to develop momentum into the throw, and also pick the easiest hop to field, thus minimizing the effects of a likely bad hop (the more hops the ball is allowed to take, the greater

Good infielding requires getting in front of the ball, getting down to be able to take the grounder at its lowest trajectory, and preparing to put the free hand over the ball to keep hold of it and then make a quick throw—keeping the mouth open is not required.
Photo courtesy of ASA

the chance that one will be bad—sort of a philosophy of life). Many infielders make the costly mistake of waiting for a routine grounder to reach them, which not only increases the chances of a bad hop, but necessitates a hurried throw. When in doubt, charge the ball. Obviously, this is of utmost importance on the slow moving ball which often must be fielded on the run and thrown in a sidearm or underhand fashion.

A school-boy's tale, the wonder of an hour of softball practice
Lord Byron
(1788-1824)
Childe Harold

Fielding balls in the Air
An important skill for all infielders to develop, and one that is often overlooked in practice, is that of running down and then catching

pop-ups and short fly balls. Generally, practices are very efficient in improving this skill, though the author was a personal witness (victim?) to one time when it was not. At the time, I was playing second base for my high school team, St. Xavier High School in Cincinnati, Ohio. As a junior I did not start regularly; however, I was lucky enough to be allowed to start against a team with many players from my home neighborhood, Newport (Kentucky) Catholic High School. It was a generous gesture by Dick Berning, my coach at the time.

However, in the warm-up he casually hit me a couple of pop-ups. Both of them went into the sun; I followed one and dropped it and completely missed the other. Trying to pick up my confidence, he hit numerous others in the same general area. However, it did little for my confidence since I had choked by this time, missed virtually all of them, and came close to gaining a concussion. By this time I was feeling very embarrassed, a feeling made all the worse by the catcalls from my friends on the other bench. After awhile he mercifully terminated this practice, pointing out that it was probably better for my own safety if I sat down and waited somewhere for the game to start. He was kind enough to allow me to go ahead and play the game and luckily I did not get any pop-ups, much to the chagrin of my opposition. I don't recall being nominated for the Golden Glove Award that year.

Has seen them fall,
One and by one,
The folk of the sun
Kissing the earth
 Hyam Plutzik
 (1911-   )
 Argumentum ad Hominem

In fielding such plays in an actual game, the infielder should be willing to be called off by other players who have a better shot at the ball. For infield pop-ups, a good rule of thumb is that shortstops always have the first call on any balls they can reasonably reach, and to call to the appropriate player for anything they realize they cannot handle. Players are then accustomed to listen for one voice, and are less likely to confuse each other with contradictory calls.

Along similar lines, outfielders should always try to field whatever short fly balls they can possibly reach behind the infield, as it is much easier to come in for a ball than to go back. On short fly balls hit behind the infield, infielders should turn their back to the plate and begin running back for the ball. The infielder who has thought ahead and anticipated this situation will already have an idea as to how far back the outfielders are playing. In any case, infielders should listen for an outfielder to call them off on such a play, as the outfielder can see both

Going for a foul ball is often one of the toughest plays for an infielder. Hustle and keeping an eye on the ball can bring about a great catch like this one.
Photo by Duane Hamamura
Courtesy of Fournier Newspapers
and the ASA

the ball and infielder. If the infielder hears nothing, then the catch should be attempted. If, on the other hand, an outfielder calls for the ball, the infielder should immediately stop, and get out of the way quickly. The need to practice on short fly balls between the infield and outfield cannot be overstated, as this is a situation which can cause injury, as well as errors. Communication between outfielders and infielders is obviously the key to a successful team play here, and outfielders in particular must learn to take charge on short fly balls just behind the infield.

It has been said . . . that there are few situations in a softball game that cannot be honourably settled, and without loss of time, either by suicide, a bag of gold, or by thrusting a despised antagonist over the edge of a precipice upon a dark night . . .
Ernest Bramah
(1868-1942)
Kai Lung's Golden Hours:
The Incredible Obtuseness . . .

Special Situations and Trick Plays

A working knowledge of common plays and situations is essential to successful infield play. One such situation, which often results in unnecessary errors in amateur softball, is the run-down play. All infielders should develop skill in dealing with a base runner trapped between the bases. Runners are often allowed to escape from apparent traps because of a poor play or because players are not backing up as they should. To avoid this, a few basic principles should be remembered.

The two infielders who initiate a run-down play should always try to move the runner back in the direction of the base the runner has just left. Usually the best way to accomplish this, particularly for infielders of better than average speed, is to run directly at the runner, forcing a return to the prior base. When the runner is no more than six steps or so from the bag, a quick toss should be made in an attempt to deliver the ball to the base first, thus allowing an easy put-out. Even if the runner sucessfully beats the throw, nothing has been lost. This is often a far better consequence than the problematic results that can occur from numerous throws involving several players.

Generally speaking, the successful run-down play involves a minimum of throws and players. Players who are not directly involved in the run-down, such as the pitcher, an outfielder, or an extra infielder, should look to back up the play. This prevents a situation in which the runner can quickly get past the infielder, allowing the runner a second chance to advance to the next base.

Two additional words of caution should also be made. Unnecessarily low throws should be avoided in run-down situations, as they are usually difficult to field and may hit the runner. Many players make the mistake of hitting the runner, even when such a throw was obviously unnecessary. Infielders should also be aware of any other runners who are on base, particularly on third, as a run-down can sometimes be used as an offensive decoy to try to divert attention and score a run.

Tag plays in general can cause problems for many softball players. The most important factor here is positioning. Whenever possible, every effort should be made to "straddle the base," which is to stand squarely facing the runner with the base between your feet. Once the throw is received, the gloved hand should be placed directly in front of the bag, with eyes focused on the runner, forcing a slide into the tag. Such a tag should be made with two hands whenever possible, and the ball should be pulled away from the runner immediately after the tag has been made. If an infielder is unable to establish a set position such as this due to a bad throw or a lack of time, the tag itself should remain the same: *low, quick,* and *firm.*

Double plays can rescue teams from many precarious situations, and are thus high on the list of special situation plays to be learned. The efficient double play requires quickness, accuracy, and timing, and as a result benefits immeasurably from the old standard, "Practice, practice, practice." The shortstop and second baseman must especially master the skills involved in turning the double play at second base. For the shortstop, the turn is best made by sliding the right foot across second base just as the throw from the right side arrives, and then relaying a quick, hard throw to first. This play is easier for shortstops if they approach second at an angle which already carries them towards first base.

For the second baseman the turn is more difficult, and may require use of either foot, depending on the angle and direction of the throw from short or third. If at all possible, the second baseman should try to tag second with the right foot, as this makes for a shorter and faster turn. For a throw that is wide and to the right, however, it may be necessary to tag the base with the left foot, then step back from the base, and complete the turn and throw. In any case, regardless of the player and base involved in a double play, the infielder should always remember that the success of the play depends on the quickness and accuracy of the throws involved. The smart infielder will always make sure of the first out, the lead runner, before completing the double play. This is especially true when the ball has been slowly hit, or is deep in the hole.

The team who is willing to put in some time to practice certain "trick plays" will often find them to be critical in a close ball game. A creative coach can come up with any number of variations on standard plays, such as the following. This relatively easy to learn play attempts a surprise "pick-off" of a fast and overanxious runner at second. Given a situation with a runner on second and less than two outs, a shortstop or third baseman can appear to fake a throw to first base on a hard grounder hit directly at them, and then turn and make a quick throw behind the runner at second, who very likely will be leaning toward third, hoping to advance on the expected throw to first. This play is even more effective with fast runners who feel they have a chance to advance to third on a throw to first from the left side of the infield. The play should be signalled beforehand, even though the appropriate ground ball will come far fewer times than not. The signal tells the second baseman to sneak in behind the runner while the shortstop or third baseman fields the ball. The fielder should avoid looking to check the runner at all, using a verbal cue from the second baseman instead, and be sure to make a good fake of the throw to first. Even though the exact situation may occur infrequently, the shock in the surprised runner's eyes will be more than worth the wait.

*I have two luxuries to brood over in my
walks, your loneliness and where to play.
that I could have possesion of both of them
in the same minute . . .*
John Keats
(1795-1921)
Letters to Fanny Brawne
8 July 1819

Infield Alignments

There are three basic infield alignments: 1) regular depth; 2) double play depth; and 3) in-tight infield depth.

In the regular infield depth alignment, the third baseman and first baseman should both play at least a few steps behind the bag and off the line, depending on the perceived abilities of the batter. If there is a strong hitting right hander who also pulls the ball, the third baseman should play deeper and move closer to the foul line. The converse is true for the first baseman when there is a lefty who pulls the ball to right. Since there is no issue of bunting or stealing in slow pitch softball, the second baseman and shortstop can play deeper and vary their positioning with greater flexibility. This deep position not only gives them greater range on ground balls, but also allows them to reach more short fly balls behind the infield. This positioning becomes especially advantageous in such situations as a runner on second with two outs. Here the infielder must make every effort to keep the ball in the infield by reaching out and knocking down any balls that are hit in the hole, thus preserving a chance to get out of the inning without allowing the runner on second to score.

In double play depth, the third baseman should play approximately even with the bag, the first baseman a step or two in front, and the shortstop and second baseman two to three steps closer to the plate and a step towards second. Second basemen should always be aware of the optimal angle for covering second on a ball hit to the left side, and take a position accordingly.

The in-tight infield alignment is typically used when there is a winning or tying run on third base. This alignment may also be used when there is a weak hitter at bat, especially if that batter is left-handed. In this case the first and third basemen should move in about four or five feet, and a step or two towards the mound. The shortstop and the second baseman should move into line with the base paths, and possibly a step or two towards second base, thus enabling the pitcher to concentrate on fielding the area in front of the pitcher's mount. Also, infielders should always take note of any particularly fast or slow runners, and adjust their fielding depth accordingly.

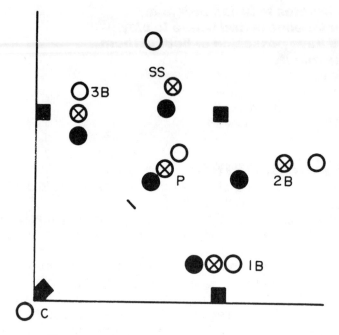

These are suggested
positions for (slow pitch)
infield depth O ; double play
depth ⊗ ; and cut-off depth
(for a play at home plate) ●

The Infield Positions

Third base is played by fools like me,
But only God can make a tree.
   (Alfred) Joyce Kilmer
   (1886-1918)
   Trees

Third Base

Third base is reasonably known as the "hot corner" in softball. Since the majority of batters are right handers and since it is relatively easy to pull the ball hard down the line, the third baseman receives many sharply hit balls that allow little time to do more than react. Thus, the position requires a certain degree of fearlessness (or insanity) that may not be as necessary for other infield positions.

Third base is not only the "hot corner" because of the hard line drives and grounders that are common there, but also because of the many tough plays that occur when a runner tries to take that extra base.
Photo by Harold Haven
Courtesy of the Chattanooga
Times and the ASA

There are also a number of other characteristics required of third basemen. They must be able to quickly recover if they manage only to knock down or stop a sharply hit ball with their body. A strong arm is very important, not only because of the issue of reacting to a stopped ball, but because the throw is a long one. A quick set of reflexes is also necessary, though speed in lateral movement is not as critical here as it is for shortstops and second basemen. When the ball is topped toward third base as a slow roller, the third baseman must come in quickly, field the ball, often with the throwing hand, and make a rapid, hard throw to first. Oftentimes this throw is a snap throw or is made underhanded, so speed and accuracy from a variety of throwing positions is required. The underhand snap throw is especially helpful on these slow hit balls, as the throw can be made in virtually the same motion that is used in fielding the ball.

Just as the ability to make throws is important, it is also important for the third baseman, as well as other infielders, to know when not to make a throw. There are many times when a ball is dropped or stopped, and once the ball is picked up, there is little chance to get the runner at first. Throwing the ball in such circumstances is a common mistake in amateur softball. The runner is seldom out, and it's quite probable that a hurried throw will go wild, thus providing extra bases for all runners. The shortstop, who has an overall perspective on such a play, can usually help here and can call out if there is no chance to get the runner at first.

The third baseman must also be ready for low pop-ups that are fouled off by the batter. Again, reaction time is important. Most high pop-ups that go behind third base are better taken by the shortstop, who will have a better angle on the ball.

If there are runners on first and second base, the third baseman should communicate ahead of time with the pitcher so that they understand how a slowly hit ball toward third will be handled. In this specific case, it is wise to allow the pitcher to do the fielding, if at all possible, with the third baseman staying on third to cover for a force play. This is in keeping with the maxim that it is critical to keep runners from advancing to second and third base in softball.

The third baseman should also watch and communicate with the pitcher on hits to right field whenever there is a possibility the runner will eventually try to go to third. The pitcher can either go into the area between second and third and back up the shortstop who is covering second base, or else move to back up the third baseman if it appears there is more likelihood of an eventual play at third base. If the pitcher does back up the third baseman, the third baseman should be ready to retrieve any wild throw that gets past the shortstop on a throw into second.

Not only must the third baseman have good reflexes and a reasonably strong arm, but also a gutsy attitude about the expected hard line shots to the chest (or even in more vulnerable areas). The third baseman has to recover quickly from these and still get off a quick and accurate throw to beat the runner. So the third baseman's rule of thumb is to first move to block a hard hit ball, possibly dropping to one knee and *always* keeping the head down, and then trying to keep the ball out in front when it cannot be fielded cleanly, and not panic on the throw.

Third basemen should play as deep down the line as the respective power and quickness of their throwing arms allow. Many balls are hit with such velocity toward third that playing deep is no disadvantage in terms of moving the ball into the throw in a reasonable amount of time. A player with a strong arm can save a lot of hits by playing back even a step or two. When third basemen note that a player likes to pull the ball hard down the line, or that the batter is standing very close to the plate and the pitcher is keeping the ball inside, they should move within a few feet of the line and cue the shortstop to move over to eliminate a wide hole between third and short. When they see that a left-handed batter is standing away from the plate, they should move in, as such a player is unlikely to hit the ball with power to left field.

In lower skill level softball leagues, a team will occasionally try to hide a weak infielder at third base. This is usually not a wise move, as it will only work against the team that does not systematically check out the defense by forcing each of them to take some chances in the early innings. Once a weak fielder at third base is discovered, he or she almost has to be moved to another position, since any right-handed batter can deliver a hard shot to the third baseman.

Another mistake in many lower skill level leagues, for third basemen as well as shortstops, is to play *too* deep, relative to level of fielding skills. They are usually modeling themselves after players who have better arms and reflexes. I have seen any number of players who make an adequate stop of the ball, though possibly including a momentary fumble, and complete an accurate throw to first only to have an average runner beat them by a step or two. An observant coach needs to move them in. It's better to sacrifice the extra hit or two that will get past them in order to make all of the sure outs.

We cannot all be shortstops, and many
Are the ways by which God leads his own
To eternal life.
Miguel De Cervantes
(1547-1616)
Don Quixote

Shortstop

Most would agree that shortstop is one of the toughest positions to play in softball. It is critical to a team's success to have a good shortstop. Like

Sometimes taking a throw at shortstop makes one very vulnerable to a hard slide. Vulnerable may be understating it a bit here.
Photo by Sun Photos
Courtesy of The Clearwater
Sun and the ASA

the third baseman, the shortstop is expected to field numerous hard, one-hop shots, while at the same time covering a great deal of territory on the left side of the field, the area where most balls are hit. The pitcher who is confident of his shortstop, and is able to consistently keep the ball on the outside of the plate with right-handed pull hitters, will enjoy a long night of ground ball outs to short.

Because of the wide variety of plays required of shortstops, they must have a diverse set of skills: the ability 1) to make exceptionally quick lateral movements in order to cover the position; 2) to charge slowly hit balls; 3) to make a stop in the hole to the backhand, and still get off a quick, hard throw; 4) to make a quick and accurate throw to second in double play situations; 5) to take a throw from the second baseman and convert it into a double play with a quick, strong relay; 6) to handle pop-ups and short flies over most of the left side of the infield, including that area behind third base; 7) to remain awake and alert so as to take the right position on relay throws from the outfield; anmd 8) to direct the flow of the game on hits to the outfield. In addition, it's great if he or she can hit the ball well, is a cordial teammate, and also provides cold refreshments after the game.

For many years I was lucky to have such a fellow in Ron "The Vacuum" Stambaugh. Not only does he fulfill the above criteria, and also is a fine clutch hitter, but Ron is an excellent potter. We periodically tried to nominate him to the Hall of Fame for potter-infielders, but we were never able to find the correct address (and he didn't look very macho wearing his cute "Little Bit o' Bybee Pottery" T-shirt). In any case, whenever we envisioned entering a team into a new league, and had a choice of nights, I would go ask Ron what nights he would have free. Whatever nights he said he had free were the nights that we picked to play. A good shortstop is that important.

Since shortstops are usually the best and most experienced fielders, they should direct most of the infield strategy, such as making sure the pitcher knows who is taking the throw at second on a double play if the ball is hit back to the mound. Shortstops should also direct their outfielders to be aware of the possible plays at second, third, or home *before* the ball is hit, and then help to direct any throws once a play is underway. They should also take charge on infield pop-ups, fielding whichever ones they can reach, and helping to call for the appropriate play on those they cannot. Generally speaking, the shortstop should act as the infield quarterback.

The shortstop also has more options on the double play than either the second or third basemen have. For example, it is almost never possible for the second baseman to field a grounder, touch second, and convert the double play alone. On the other hand, shortstops in many instances should skip flipping the ball to the second baseman and instead stride across the bag and go ahead and complete the play alone. The movement to pick up the ball near second base gives them both the momentum and the correct angle for the throw. The general rule of thumb is to consider this option on any ball hit to the shortstop's left.

These types of plays are the kind that demand communication between the second baseman and shortstop. It is ideal if a team can have a second base-shortstop combination that has played together for some period of time, as many plays require both an immediate response and a clear knowledge of what the other person will do. For example, when second basemen must go deep to their right to field a ground ball, sometimes requiring a diving or off-balance catch, they may choose to flip the ball underhand to their shortstop, who is gathering momentum toward first base by the movement toward the ball. This is not a double play, but the same movement allows the shortstop to get off a quicker and stronger throw than the second baseman could, even though there is no touching second base at all. Obviously, such a play requires some experience together, and the play itself should be practiced many times.

Shortstops do have to be careful of the runner coming into second base on double plays. Since the momentum is toward first base, shortstops are especially vulnerable to injury from being taken out by any hard sliding (and sometimes sadistic) runners. Quickness is the key factor here. Shortstops should concentrate on making a quick, sweeping tag of second base with the right foot, at the same time throwing to first. Momentum will carry the fielder away from the bag, and the runner who still insists on "taking him out," should be called for interference (if not beaten into quivering jelly with broken bats—a primitive, nevertheless, satisfying ritual).

Shortstops, as well as second basemen, confront a real dilemma whenever runners on an opposing team, either through ignorance or misguided courage, come into second base standing up, or otherwise try to disrupt a double play by flapping their arms, shouting, and so on. The humane course of action is to hold the ball if it appears likely that the throw would hit the runner, and then appeal to the umpire for an interference call. The good umpire quickly gives the call, since to do otherwise would encourage more of the same, and many fielders would then start making the dangerous throw. Such a throw, while certainly not sportsmanlike, does get the message across. At one time one of my teammates continually insisted on going into second base standing up on double plays, and purposely interfering with the throw. Unfortunately, for some period of time he was not called for interference, so his belief that he was being effective was reinforced. Then, one shortstop decided that this was simply too much and released the ball in a strong throw just as Jim was coming into second base waving his arms. The ball caught him squarely in the forehead and he went down as if he had been pole-axed. After recovering from the concussion and fifteen stitches, Jim went into second base with a lot more caution and good sense.

Finally, shortstops should always be aware of base coverage on hits to the outfield. Generally, they should take the cut-off throw from the left and left center fielders, and cover second base on hits to right and right center. They should also be prepared to cover second base whenever the second baseman has to move to cover first base. As always, good communication is the crucial variable in plays such as these.

***A foul fiend is coming over
the infield to meet him;
his name is Apollyon.***
> John Bunyan
> (1628-1688)
> *The Pilgrim's Progress*

Second Base

Second base requires many of the skills typically associated with shortstop, including the coverage of second base, good lateral mobility and quickness, and the ability to turn the double play. The one clear lesser requirement lies in the shorter distance required for the throw. As a result, the second baseman should rival the shortstop's range and mobility, but does not need to have an equally strong throwing arm.

Because of the short, quick throw required in most plays, the second baseman often has the luxury of having plenty of time to complete a put-out, even after a ball has been fumbled, or a particularly fast runner is going to first. Such plays can be very worthwhile to practice. Have balls thrown or batted to you on the ground and purposely boot them, or look away at the last second and allow an error, and then practice responding to your error to get a sense of the behaviors needed for the pickup and recovery throw. Such a throw will often be of a quick, underhand type, and may have to be made from an off-balance position. This type of throw must be mastered by the second baseman, as it will also be required after charging a slowly hit ground ball or completing a double play at second base. The key point in making a recovery from a bobbled ball is to keep your eye on the ball instead of paying attention to where the runner is. At the same time be aiert for verbal cues from your teammates as to where the ball should be thrown. Do not try to split your attention between the ball and the runner, as this will usually result in more fumbles.

Like shortstops, the second baseman must be aware of the responsibilities for covering second base on infield and outfield plays. Typically, the second baseman should cover second base on a double play for balls hit to short or third, or back to the pitcher by a pull hitting right-handed batter who has caused the shortstop to shift towards third.

The second baseman's turn at second is a difficult one, and requires extensive practice to master the skills involved. Check the earlier subsection on double plays for more information in this regard. For balls hit to the outfield, the second baseman should be prepared to take relay throws on hits to right field and right center, and to cover second on balls hit to left and left center. Also, the second baseman often has a specific duty to take pop-ups hit directly behind first base, as it is easier to move laterally than to have to turn and run back for the ball.

The loam gleams like wet coal;
the Green, the springing green
Makes an intenser day
and a tough infield.
  Theodore Roethke
  (1908-   )
  Words for the Wind

The turn required at second base can put the second baseman in a precarious position. A short step into the infield as the throw is made helps eliminate this.
Photo by Manuello A. Ovalles
Courtesy of ASA

The second baseman should play very deep in the infield in most situations (except when the field is very wet), even moving into the outfield grass on most standard softball diamonds. The fact that the second baseman, as well as the other infielders, can do this reflects the major difference between slow-pitch softball and baseball or fast-pitch softball. Infielders in slow-pitch softball have no need to worry about a stolen base or a bunt. Thus whenever it is strategic to do so they can play very deep. In actuality, most second basemen do not play as deep as they should or could. The coach should note if they are making put outs with the luxury of taking their time on the pick up and throw and then beating the runner by several steps. If this happens with any consistency whatsoever, it indicates that the second baseman is playing too shallow, relative to his or her athletic abilities. Playing deeper allows much more range on ground balls, much more time to react to ground balls and line drives, and greater coverage of shallow pop flies into right field.

A wise and masterly inactivity.
T'is first base.
John Randolph
(1773-1833)
Speeches (1828)

First Base

First basemen should be tall, even if they are inclined to be a bit slow. The tall first baseman can save many put outs over the course of a long season that a shorter player simply would not be able to reach. Particularly in amateur softball, where the quality of throws to first from the infield may vary greatly, a tall and rangy first baseman will have a distinct advantage in offering a higher and wider target for the infielders, a quality they always appreciate.

First basemen should play as far back down the line as possible. They may also wish to move away from the line, depending on whether the batter is left or right-handed, whether the batter has been known to pull the ball, the lateral movement ability of the second baseman, etc. In any case, first basemen should still remain within a distance where they can get to first base and perform their primary task, which is taking the throw from the other infielders, in a well set position. Some first basemen play too far away from first base and end up taking the throws from the other infielders when they are off-balance or are reaching for the bag. This has three drawbacks. First of all, it is disrupting to the other infielders, who may hesitate on a throw and subsequently make a poor one. Secondly, if the throw is at all wide, the first baseman's range of reach is restricted by any off-balance position. Thirdly, he or she can very well miss the base because of trying to attend to the throw from the infield. Generally speaking, first basemen should try to get to first base while a

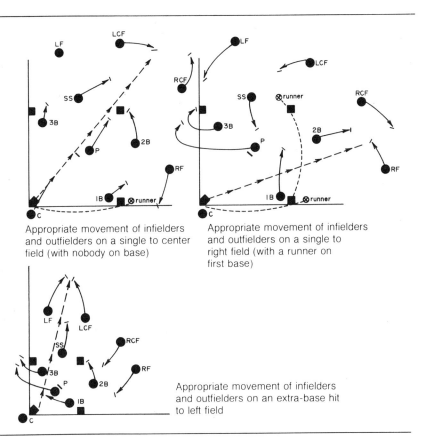

Appropriate movement of infielders and outfielders on a single to center field (with nobody on base)

Appropriate movement of infielders and outfielders on a single to right field (with a runner on first base)

Appropriate movement of infielders and outfielders on an extra-base hit to left field

A representative sample of the appropriate positions and movements for infielders and outfielders

ball is still being fielded in the infield. Lefthanded first basemen will typically do this by anchoring the left foot on the base and stretching with the right one, while the converse is true for the right-handed player.

One play which often causes confusion in an infield is the ground ball between the first and second basemen which both may move to field, thus requiring an unusually alert and quick pitcher to cover first base in time to make a play. The general rule of thumb for the first baseman is to only attempt to field those balls hit to your right which are within a step or two of your position. Let the second baseman worry about the rest, and move to cover first as quickly as possible.

A demonstration of excellent form at first base—stretching out to take the throw while keeping the foot on the edge of the base, and holding the low throw in with the free hand, while blocking the ball with the body.
Photo by Bob Mack
Courtesy of the Nashville
Banner and the ASA

The Outfield

Gather ye the fly balls while ye may
   Old Time is a-flying
And this same high fly, that smiles today
   To-morrow will fall in . . .
     Robert Herrick
     (1591-1674)
     To the Virgins to
     make much of Time

Playing the outfield defensively at least appears to be a relatively simple task. In essence, you stand around with a degree of attention until the ball is hit towards you and then go for it and do your best to catch it on the fly or at least stop it. In that vein, some coaches seem to feel that outfielders are those individuals, who though at least athletically able, are not well versed in the specific skills that would allow them to play the infield. However, playing the outfield well requires a number of characteristics: obviously, 1) the ability to catch the ball; but also 2) good speed in all directions; 3) the ability to judge sinking line balls and decide whether to make the catch or simply to stop the ball; 4) the ability to go back quickly on a ball hit directly over one's head while still retaining visual contact with it and then catching it; 5) a good, strong arm for throwing to the bases; and 6) the ability to stay alert even though one may have little direct involvement in the game for significant periods of time.

The latter characteristic is hard to teach, and requires of outfielders a level of concentration that is not reinforced by the degree of involvement in the game that most infielders enjoy. As noted earlier in this section, this level of concentration is easier to maintain when the team has a good pitcher who gets the first couple of pitches into the strike zone, as this forces a more continuous sequence of action. Pitchers who persistently run the count to something like three balls and one or two strikes before the batter has to swing and hit the ball risk losing the alertness of their fielders, and especially the outfielders. In many instances, one can observe the fielders, especially outfielders, gradually becoming disinterested bystanders. As life would have it, it is also usually just at that moment that someone puts a solid line drive into one of the outfield alleys. In any case, a low level of alertness results in a slow start on the ball, making it easier for a ball to fall in fair when it would have otherwise been an out.

He maketh me to play in green outfields . . .
Psalm xxiii. 2.

Communication

Playing the outfield does not simply require running to the ball and catching it or stopping it without any consideration for other issues. The outfielder does have a number of communication concerns. First, in many instances a pop up or fly ball is potentially catchable by another outfielder or one or more infielders. There should be some attention to this communication issue before the game so that the outfielders know who gets to make the primary call or who is to swing away if both make the call for the ball.

Outfielders ought to mentally rehearse where they will be throwing the ball if it is hit to them before each play, or at least be generally aware of probable developing situations.

74

On a ball hit between two outfielders, the best (most experienced, strongest arm, etc.) fielder is allowed the option of calling for the ball, with the assumption that the other player will veer away at his or her call. Also, it is traditional for an outfielder to have the call over an infielder. This is for good reason since outfielders will have a better judgment of where both they and the infielders are in relation to the ball, and if the outfielder can make the catch, he or she will have momentum going toward the infield and any base runners. On the other hand, the infielder will be moving away from the other runners, making it easier for them to advance. Also, it's just much easier to catch a ball while running in toward it rather than while retreating backwards, and there is less chance of falling down as one goes forward rather than backward.

Outfielders ought to also mentally rehearse where they will be throwing the ball if it is hit to them before each play, or at least be generally aware of probable developing situations. They should then fluidly move into that throwing motion as they make the catch, yet remain alert for cues from the infield as to where to throw the ball. Again, the effective team is one on which everyone knows who has the responsibility for making such calls. There is nothing like making a play in the outfield and hearing three different bases called for by various infielders, and trying immediately to guess which call might be relevant.

In softball, the ground rules vary markedly from league to league and field to field. The good umpire discusses these with the coach ahead of time, and it is especially worthwhile to at least have the left and right fielder listening in on such a discussion. In any case, the coach should make a point of letting all the outfielders, as well as the whole team, know what the ground rules are. For example, in many parks there is a line over which any balls caught are simply out of play rather than outs. If the outfielder knows that ground rule, he or she may be able to stop short of the line, lean over, catch the ball, and make it an out rather than simply having it result in a caught though dead ball.

Alternatively, when preparing to field a ball in foul territory, the outfielder should be aware of whether or not it is worthwhile to catch the ball. There may be a situation in a late inning when the game is tied and a runner is on third base with one out, and catching a long fly ball would almost automatically score the run. In such a case, it might be more strategically advantageous to allow the ball to drop foul or out of play, and then try to get the batter out in a manner that will prevent the run from scoring.

The Grand Throw

While infielders can mess up an outfielder's throw by a bad call, one of the major mistakes that outfielders make is to take a shot at the "grand throw." Such throws are indulged in whenever possible by certain outfielders with good strong arms, whose throws are nevertheless erratic on many occasions.

I played for some years with a gifted outfielder whose apparent sole joy in life was to make the grand throw. He had burning speed and would seem to catch balls that were way behind his reach. He was usually a valuable player, yet there were at least one or two plays a game when he would get his chance at the grand throw. This was usually after he bobbled a ball for an instant and the runner would try for an extra base. He knew well that he had the strong arm. However, it would take both a perfect throw by him and a perfect play by the baseman to make the out. Such a confluence of events is relatively rare in amateur softball. Nevertheless, in spite of the pleas of his teammates, he would launch his grand throw. Probably his grandest throw of all attempted to throw a runner out at the plate. Though this field had a very high backstop, he managed to clear it by a good twenty feet. While aesthetically it was beautiful, somewhat like a missile in flight, it didn't do much good for our team. Also, grand throws almost always violate one of the cardinal rules of good softball strategy, which is, keep any runners from advancing to second base.

Stance

Most outfielders feel that they can be optimally prepared for play by taking a slightly crouched position with the legs spread well apart and not locked, and with the weight of the body distributed evenly on the balls of the feet. If the ball is hit very deep, the outfielder should pivot on the foot farthest from the ball when taking the first step toward the ball. It is most important to then try to keep an eye on the ball and run toward and then under it. There may be occasions when it is impossible to keep an eye directly on the ball. In such cases, the outfielder can fix a mental image of where the ball is going, run toward that, and then look back in the direction from where it is expected. If the ball is hit to the left or right, the outfielder should pivot on one foot toward the ball and use the other foot for leverage to get a quick start.

While catching a ball on the run is more spectacular, outfielders who can get a quick start and get under the ball to make the catch are far more effective because they can set up more quickly and as a result fire a quick throw with much more power. If there is the chance to at least set up slightly before catching a fly ball, it's best to catch the ball and at the same time initially move into a stride toward the infield.

It may seem like old fashioned advice to say that all players (not just outfielders) should, if at all possible, catch the ball with one hand, then immediately cover it with the other. However, it doesn't take watching many softball games to see why such advice is still effective. As in all other phases of the game, it really is critical to keep one's eye on the ball until it is cleanly in the glove. Allow a slight give as the ball comes into the

By running back while keeping his eye on the ball, by looking over his shoulder, and then pivoting to let his back and buttocks take the brunt of the crash against the fence, Bill Huff of Barstow, California makes a great catch.
Official U.S. Marine Corps
Photo—Photo courtesy
of ASA

glove, especially on line drives, and then move the arm into the forward motion already generated by your forward step.

77

All the world's a softball field
And all the men and women merely players . . .
William Shakespeare
(1564-1616)
As You Like It

Positioning

Coaches should instruct their outfielders at the beginning of the game on the depth that they should play with various hitters, hopefully based on some advanced scouting of the opposition team. A general rule is that it is worthwhile to play outfielders a bit shallow at the start of the game (except for obvious power hitters) and challenge opposing players to hit over the outfielders. Then, if there are base runners, the outfielders should play a bit deeper to avoid allowing a ball to get through or over their heads, thus creating a big rally. This can be modified if apparently weak hitters are at bat.

Later in the game, if their team is ahead by several runs, outfielders should play relatively shallow and challenge players if they want to cut off a succession of singles that can lead to a big rally. Even if they play shallow and one big hit goes over their heads, the game is not at risk. If the game is very close, they are advised to play deeper, unless there are runners on base, at which point they might choose to play more shallow hoping to keep runners from scoring. On situations where there is one out, a single runner on third base, and the game is reasonably close, fielders should play relatively shallow in order to gain the chance to be able to throw out the runner at the plate or to prevent a score from third on a fly ball.

The corner outfielders (the right fielder and left fielder) should be particularly alert to the batter's position in the batter's box and their pitcher's tendencies and/or ability to place the ball. For example, if the right fielder sees that a right-handed batter is crowding the plate, and also knows that the pitcher can put the ball consistently on the inside part of the plate, he or she should play shallow since it's probable that the batter will not be able to hit to right field with any power. The opposite situation, of course, applies to the left fielder.

Most outfielders develop a sense of how effective they are on charging short fly balls and sinking line drives versus retrieving balls hit deeper than they are playing. Some outfielders are almost totally inept at the latter, but do a good job of charging the ball. They should be allowed to play a bit deeper than one would normally expect the average outfielder to play, and vice versa if one has a special skill in going back on the ball.

Overall, the batter's stance can be an important cue for each and every defensive player. For example, a batter who takes a regular

The sinking line drive is one of the toughest plays an outfielder can face. Keeping an eye on the ball is critical to making the play successfull.
Photo courtesy of ASA

stance, (with both feet squared up to the plate) is likely to hit directly away. For instance, a right-handed batter will hit the ball into left center field. If, however, that right-handed batter has pulled the left foot somewhat away from the plate, leaving the right foot squared up, they are likely to pull the ball to left field. Batters are also likely to pull to left field to the degree that they stand back in the box. Conversely, to the degree they stand toward the front of the plate they are likely to push it to right field, and to the degree they move the forward foot closer to the plate than the back foot, they are also likely to hit it to right field (if right-handed).

Fielders should also take note of the grip on the bat. If a bat is choked up, that is, grasped some four to six inches up the handle, the batter is sacrificing power for control and is likely at most to hit only a short fly ball. Similarly, when batters keep their hands spread wide apart on the bat, they are trying to push or chop the ball, and are not likely to hit with any power. If there has been a chance to observe the batter's swing, this can also provide some tips. Batters who tend to drop their right shoulder (for a right-handed batter, and/or the bat tip is held quite low) are very likely to hit under the ball and possibly golf it into a high fly ball. If, however, the arms and the bat tip are held relatively high, they are more likely to hit a

79

ground ball or line drive since they will be swinging down into the ball. If the arms are held close to the body and the batter is in a very crouched position, it's probable that any good hit will be a fly ball.

In most situations, the outfielder should be very aggressive in attempting to catch short fly balls and sinking line drives. The only real exception is when a ball is hit down either the third or first base lines, as it is unlikely that the other fielders will be able to provide any immediate backup if the ball is missed. But, in general, the aggressive approach does pay off. For one thing, even if the ball appears uncatchable at the last minute, the outfielder can try to take it on the short hop. On a rough playing field, this is actually an advantage since the first bounce is the only one with any high probability of being a true bounce. Of course, this strategy does require a lot of hussle and alertness on all outfielders so that the back-up is always provided.

Children of the future age
Reading this indignant page
Know that in a former time
Too much softball was thought a crime.
William Blake
(1757-1827)
A Little Girl Lost

Practice

As with any other position, practice and lots of it results in a good outfielder. Even individuals who are relatively slow and/or who do not have markedly strong arms can be adequate outfielders if they have practiced enough so that they can play with good sense and not drop any balls that they are able to get to. The more experience that players have with outfielding, either through practice and/or actual game play, the more likely that they can be "off with the pitch" as the ball is hit. This is, of course, facilitated by staying alert, as mentioned earlier, even when one has not been in on many plays. Good outfielding means that the person has developed a sense of where the ball is going to go immediately upon it's being hit. This ability is heightened to the degree that one observes the pitcher and sees where a pitch is going before it is swung at, as well as developing a sense of where individual batters like to hit the ball. The combination of alertness, experience, and observation allows a player to get a quick start on the ball and retrieve many fly balls that would otherwise fall in for hits.

It's important to use practice times to learn to make difficult plays, and one of the most difficult plays for outfielders is the pursuit of fly balls over their head. Unfortunately, when most outfielders practice, they set it up so that they are receiving relatively casual fly balls. Most people handle those well. It's the difficult ones that are needed in practice. In catching a long ball over one's head, the first step is to turn, run, and keep the ball in visible range over the shoulder. It's true that most people cannot run as fast while keeping the ball in sight over a shoulder. Yet, losing sight of the ball for even a split second quickly leads to confusion and commonly results in an error or missed catch. Only with years of experience do outfielders seem to be able to turn, run, and then pick up sight of the ball later after they have made a strong run in he general direction they feel the ball was going. An outfielder should never back pedal on a long fly ball. First, it is a slow and inefficient way of moving. Secondly, one is very prone to fall down (usually not in a very dignified manner), especially since the outfield on many amateur softball fields is generously described as "hilly terrain."

Most good outfielders realize that they will have to learn to adjust to various light conditions, and that practice under such conditions is very helpful. For example, when playing during daylight hours, learning to shade the eyes and yet keep track of the ball is an important skill to learn. Similarly, games played at night present a variety of challenging lighting conditions. Some have a high level of glare while others provide a low level of visibility. When players see that they will have to play a game under such conditions, they ought to try to at least gain some practice before the game in pursuing fly balls under these lights.

Even in the best of leagues, lighting conditions may be tough for infielders, and especially for the outfielders.
Photo courtesy of ASA

And out of the glove as soon as out of sight.
Fulke Greville, Lord Brooke
Sonnet LVI

Errors

All outfielders occasionally make physical errors in throwing. These are the results of their level of experience, their physical and psychological states in that particular play, and various physical limitations. Most of these physical errors are eliminated by the effective use of cut-off relays in the throwing pattern. Fortunately, anyone with minimal athletic skills can make an adequate and quick throw to a relay infielder who has come out within one hundred to one hundred and fifty feet of the play.

The real problems in outfielding are often the mental errors. As noted earlier, the major strategy should always be to place the throw to eliminate advances to second and third base. If outfielders on either side of the playing field adopt the strategy of throwing to the cut-off person each and every time, very few mental errors will result. However, except in cases when a runner on third is the winning run in a late inning, outfielders should never throw to home plate if there are less than two outs. This easily allows other runners to advance, which eliminates the chances for force outs and sets up the possibility of a long rally.

It's true that this conservative approach will allow an extra run to score from third base. However, in the long run this should cut off the development of any undeserved rallies. The manager should make sure that the outfielders understand ahead of the game what the throwing strategy will be. If a player then persists in violating this rule, he or she should be replaced in the line-up or at least be moved to a position, such as catcher, where such impulsive behavior will not wreak havoc on the team's chances.

Outfielders should also return the ball as quickly as possible to the infield. Some outfielders like to challenge the runner by holding the ball and faking several throws as if to say "go ahead and try it." The difficulty is that while they are doing this, the player usually advances a few steps each time and the outfielder has lost the momentum gained while running toward the ball and preparing to throw in the first place. Thus, a situation in which a runner never could have successfully advanced is changed into one where there is at least a solid probability that the advance will be successful. In my experience, the runner wins most of these "challenge" situations, and in almost all such cases the runner had no chance of originally making that extra base.

There are others so continually in the
agitation of gross and merely sensual
pleasures, or so occupied in the low
drudgery of avarice, or so heated in
the chase of honors and distinction,
that their minds, which had been used
continually to the storms of these
violent and tempestuous passions, can
hardly be put in motion by the delicate
and refined play of a softball game.
    Edmund Burke
    (1729-1792)
    On The Sublime and
    Beautiful

Outfield Defensive Alignments

There are two basic outfield defensive alignments. These are (1) the four outfielders alignment and (2) the three outfielders and a short fielder alignment, the latter which is referred to here as a three outfielder alignment. Variations based on how deep the various infielders and outfielders play can be imposed on these two basic alignments.

In general, the four outfielder alignment is preferred in most softball skill classifications, and especially at the intermediate and upper skill levels. Since hitters are much more powerful on upper level teams, and are also better able to place the ball, there is more need to eliminate any chance of their hitting the ball between the outfielders.

Some coaches have argued that the three outfielder alignment is almost worthless, stating that the short fielder is unlikely to catch more than an occasional line drive, and that most short flys that are caught would probably be handled by one of the outfielders or by a good second baseman or shortstop. Such coaches note that a good fielding pitcher should handle the ground balls (and many of the line drives) that are the usual responsibility of the short fielder if he or she plays in a line with center field.

However, a good coach, even those with upper skill level teams, can occasionally make good use of the three outfielder alignment. For one thing, no team should ever consider that they are committed to one alignment or the other for the whole game, or even for a whole inning. It's true that the four outfielder alignment is most important when dealing with hitters with good power to the outfield, or hitters who can place line shots down the lines. At the same time, almost every team, even good teams, have a couple of people who do not hit with power, and who depend on hitting sharp line drives or hard grounders through the infield. Bringing the fourth outfielder in as a fifth infielder behind the

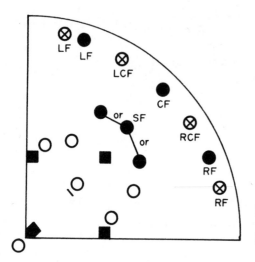

Placement of outfielders
in slow pitch.
● three deep outfielders
and one short fielder
⊗ four deep outfielders

pitcher allows a greater spread toward the lines and a closing of gaps in the infield. This forces such batters to try to hit with the power they don't have. Of course, this works best when a team has three quick outfielders. I have seen upper level teams effectively use three fleet outfielders in this alignment for substantial parts of the game.

As noted, the effectiveness of certain teams can be nullified by the three outfielder alignment (scouting helps here). In this vein, I once managed a team who happened to be paired against a team composed mainly of middle and late adolescents. These boys played ball for a neighborhood center, and when they took the field, it looked as if they simply weren't old enough to compete with the other teams in this league. Steve Riggert, a strong hitting 6'7", 240 pound outfielder (who also happens to be a very kind and gentle person) seemed embarrassed at the idea of playing them. He stated, "It's just not fair to make them play in this kind of league." Most of the other players on our team had the same attitude and assumed we would wipe them off the field within an inning or two. I was a bit more dubious since I had come early to the park, had watched them work out, and had been impressed by the slick fielding skills and strong hitting they showed in practice. I also remembered my own experience of working in a Cincinnati neighborhood center in which the kids played softball *all day*. After a few years of this, they were very skilled, though still young.

In any case, as our game progressed, we found ourselves a couple of runs·behind. Everybody on our team attributed this to "a bad day," "that lousy umpire," and/or "a lack of concentration." The actual fact is that this team was exceptionally talented defensively, using their youth and speed to full advantage. They did not have great power offensively, but were adept at slashing line drives over the head of our pitcher and through the infield holes. By the fifth inning, we had fallen six runs behind, and it became clear to me (though this may strike the reader as relatively slow learning) that this team only had one real power hitter, and that the other batters depended on hitting line drives through holes in the infield.

At this point, we changed to a three outfielder alignment, with the fifth infielder now being positioned behind second base and slightly toward the left field area. The pitcher would move back and slightly toward the right field area after delivering the ball. We, in effect, now had a six person infield in terms of areas that we could cover effectively. This closed down their offense, though we could not make up the difference in runs and lost the game by two runs. However, in a rematch several weeks later, we started with the three fielder alignment and were able to beat them by four runs. Incidentally, in this game we would switch to a four outfielder alignment for their power hitter. Any coach should be willing to quickly made these kinds of switches. Also, there should be practice with both alignments, so that players feel comfortable making the switch quickly.

Since the majority of hitters are right-handed, the left fielder is usually the most critical position in the outfield alignment. Playing left field does not require an especially strong arm, though throws must be at least accurate. It is very helpful if the left fielder (and in fact, all the outfielders) takes an aggressive attitude in the field, by trying to catch low sinking line drives. This means that the left center fielder will have to be ready to quickly back-up the play. Left fielders should also be the most skilled in going back and retrieving balls hit over their heads since this is most likely to occur in left field.

Some have argued that the right fielder should be the team's third best outfielder, rather than weakest outfielder, as so often is the case. This is debatable and, of course, depends upon the hitting style of the opposition. My own feeling is that right field, rather than right center, demands more skill, in part because many of the plays present substantial difficulty even though there is little likelihood of being quickly backed up by another outfielder. Secondly, the right fielder has the longest throw to third base, and additionally many of the better right-handed power hitters are becoming more skilled at hitting to right field, thus putting a premium on the ability to effectively cover that position. So my own preference (usually) is to put the weakest outfielder in right center, the two strongest fielders in left and left center, and the third best outfielder in right field.

The prior several parts of this section of the book have focused on the defense. We now turn to the most important aspects of the offense, batting and base running, and we'll then finish off this section with a consideration of the need for blending it all together through coaching.

I'll make thee famous by my glove
And glorious by my bat.
James Graham
First Marquis of Montrose
(1612-1650)
from his song,
"My Dear and only Love"

Batting

The bat is mightier than the sword.
Edward Bulwer Lytton
(1805-1873)
Richelieu

Factors in Batting Success

"Like the pitcher and catcher on defense, the softball hitter must live with the knowledge that this whole game has been concocted to make his task easy. It is this knowledge, I think, that causes one to lunge and overswing at the plate, that causes one's concentration to collapse just as that big, fat, ridiculous target comes drifting up before one's eyes. Patience, poise, concentration, a continuous view of the ball, a loose and level swing—all this is imperative; as a hitter you must be humble, respect the game, and maintain all the fundamentals. Swing for ground balls before pop-ups, and line drives before long, high flies. Let the other team make the difficult play" (Slote, 1982, p. 18).

As is evident in this quote from John Slote a variety of factors can contribute to batting success. There are many factors in addition to those he mentions, including general athletic ability and overall body mass. However, the three major factors that lead to continuing success in batting are *concentration, consistency,* and *practice.*

The old maxim "keep your eye on the ball" is testimony to the early recognition of the important role that concentration plays in developing hitting skills. Just as with the perfect shot in golf or tennis, the well hit softball occurs when the player's eyes follow the ball until it connects with the bat. Techniques for improving this skill are detailed in the next section on playing the game better. Fortunately, unlike baseball, the ball is pitched so slowly in slow pitch softball that most batters can actually see this contact.

Consistency here refers to the ability to develop an easy, natural swing, and then stay in that rhythm each time one bats. Professional ball players help to achieve this by periodically taking video tapes of themselves swinging, and then checking for deviations from their standard pattern. This is particularly valuable when players are in a "slump," since they can make a detailed check as to how they made the swing when they were hitting well.

The softball player can obviously use video tape equipment too, and this is recommended whenever possible. However, keeping a checklist in one's mind of the things that are important also works effectively (and more cheaply) to keep the batter's swing in a consistent pattern. This checklist would at least include 1) keeping one's eye on the ball; 2) swinging straight "through" the ball; 3) shifting one's weight from the

back foot to the front foot as the swing is made; 4) getting the power and weight of the whole body into the swing; and 4) snapping the wrist just about the time the ball is hit.

Another helpful practice is the use of mental imagery, which in this case would involve the repetitive imagining of a perfect, successful swing. Imagery training in general is discussed in the last overall section in this book, and it can be particularly helpful for improving batting skills. As is noted in that section, it is important to always image the *optimal* swing, to rehearse it in one's mind consistently, and then to "connect" that rehearsal with an actual swing as one is preparing to hit while in the batters' box.

As implied by the preceeding discussion of mental imagery, practice is important. While practice can be in the form of mental imagery, it must eventually be translated into actual batting situations. It's ironic that so many softball practices consist of a lot of work on defensive skills, while only involving a few practice swings at a ball being thrown by anyone willing to pitch (usually pitching quickly, and with little regard for a strike zone). For this reason, as well as others, it has been my experience that a more beneficial method of practicing is a form of an intrasquad practice game. Twelve people, for example, are divided into four teams of three (offensive teams, while all others play in the field while one team of three is at bat), with the team pitcher(s) pitching against all teams. Each team alternately takes their turn at bat, with each team getting three outs, and players can be rotated through various defensive positions as well.

A hit! A hit! My kingdom for a hit.
William Shakespeare
(1564-1616)
King Richard III

Batting Stance

While consistency in batting form is important in batting success, the exact aspects of the stance may be altered, depending on the particular situation. However, even when making these shifts, the batters should keep the general form as consistent as possible.

Beyond a few general techniques, the "ideal" batting form is the one that happens to get the job done. And there are almost as many different swings as there are players. I recall as a young boy that I virtually adored Stan Musial, the star outfielder for the St. Louis Cardinals during that era. Musial was a truly great hitter, but had a very unusual stance in which he twisted himself up like a corkscrew, with his bat pointing straight up to the sky. As many youngsters do at that phase of development, I tried to emulate everything about him, including his batting stance. Unfortunately, while it worked for him, it didn't for me, and left me with a low batting average and a very stiff neck.

No matter what stance the batter takes, he or she should feel comfortable and loose at the plate. Many batters have various rituals that they go through to try to achieve this looseness, and the mental imagery techniques discussed later in this book are helpful here. As touched on earlier, the fundamental "do's" of hitting are 1) keeping your eye on the ball so that optimal contact can be made; 2) shifting one's weight from the back foot to the front foot as the swing is made; 3) snapping the wrists just about the time the ball is hit; 4) swing straight "through" the ball with arms fully extended; and 5) getting the power and weight of the whole body into the swing.

Many players find it helpful to twist their whole torso, including the upper parts of their legs to their right a bit (assuming a right-handed hitter), and then as the ball approaches the plate, to start to twist back. This helps produce an extra amount of momentum to go along with the stride into the ball off the back foot. This is followed by attempting to meet the ball in front of the body, with a full follow-through. In meeting the ball slightly out in front of the body, the batter gets maximum impact by harnessing the power of the wrist snap, as well as from the momentum built up by the body twist and the forward stride.

The positioning of a batter in the batter's box can vary along two major dimensions: Close or Away; and Short or Deep.

In most situations the best position is to stand away from home plate and deep in the box. This helps the batter with the high and inside strike, a type of strike that many players commonly have difficulty with. The batter who consistently stands short in the batter's box (closer to the pitcher) is vulnerable to any pitch with a high loft. Such a ball has to be hit high in the shoulder area, which reduces the power of the swing greatly. It often results in undercutting the ball, which in turn produces an easy out pop fly. By standing deep in the batter's box, the batter gets an extra second to allow the high arc pitch to drop further, and thus the ball can be hit after it has come well below shoulder level. A batter who stands relatively close to the plate is vulnerable to the inside pitch since it is difficult to get the "heart" of the bat on the ball. By standing relatively away from the plate, the batter can make better contact on such a pitch.

Since the strike zone technically is from the batter's knees up to shoulder height when standing relatively erect, most balls must fall about 3 to 6 inches behind the plate (depending on the size of the player) to technically be strikes. However, most umpires have developed the habit of calling anything a strike that plops down just behind the plate in an acceptable arc. With such umpires, batters may have to move slightly more forward in the batter's box to avoid being vulnerable to the low and outside pitch. Batters who are unable to deliver power to the opposite field may also need to stand a bit closer to the plate so as to capitalize on any chance to pull the ball.

Umpires also vary in how much arc they require on a pitch. The rules say the pitch must be between 6 and 12 feet at the peak of its arc. In actuality, I have found umpires to generally accept a range more like 5 to 10 feet. If a batter is consistently receiving pitches with less than 7 or 8 feet of arc, he will need to move up a bit toward the pitcher in the batter's box, while staying reasonably away from the plate. This allows a swing at the ball before it gets so low that the ball is either "golfed" or chopped, producing a pop fly or easy grounder, respectively.

Most power hitters, such as Abe Baker of Providence, Rhode Island, grip the bat at the end so as to get greater leverage, and thus more power, into a hit.
Photo courtesy of ASA

Batters who stand relatively away and deep in the box should be able to obtain one or more good pitches to hit each time at bat. Possibly the worst position to take in the batting box is to crowd the plate. Some batters seem to feel that this will intimidate a pitcher into providing a base on balls. Little do they realize, however, that a good pitcher loves such a stance. Pitchers simply place the ball high and inside, and the batter either takes this obviously difficult-to-hit pitch for a strike, or is likely to foul the ball off. In any case, it is very easy for the batter who stands close to the plate to get behind in the count at 0 and 2, and then have to deal with pitches that are going to be even more difficult to hit.

***There is a homely adage which runs
'Speak softly and carry a big stick;
you will go far!'***
President Theodore Roosevelt
(1858-1919)
at the Minnesota State Fair
2 Sept. 1901

Bat Position

The manner in which the bat is held can also be an important factor in batting success. The bat is held with both hands, one above the other, with the hand of the arm closest to the pitcher at the bottom of the bat. The majority of players position their hands flush against one another, though some players separate their hands slightly, claiming that this gives them more bat control. In terms of placement of the hands on the bat, there are three general positions. Most players make the grip at the very end of the bat. This grip is effective for power hitting, but is less useful for placing the ball. At the other extreme is the "choking-up" grip, in which the batter moves the hands up as much as five or six inches from the end of the bat. This provides increased bat control at the expense of power. In between the long and the choke grips is something creatively termed the "medium" grip. This allows the batter to have better bat control than the long grip and more power than the choking-up grip. The proper grip to use depends on the player's skill, power, and particular game situations.

Choking up gives more bat control for place-hitting, though there is less power available to the batter.
Photo by Paul Salmon

The Ball

Developing a good hitting attack in a game may even depend on the ball itself. Softballs have certainly attained a quality and uniformity unknown in the days when George Hancock introduced a lace-bound boxing glove as the first ball. However, there are still marked differences among manufactured softballs, even the official types. They differ primarily in how well they hold their shape, how quickly they become badly scuffed or ripped at the seams, and most importantly, they differ in how "active" they are (how far they go when hit).

Those differences are reflected in price, and buying a softball that is cheap in price means getting one that is likely to be cheap in performance. One slugger on my early teams, Jim McGovern, used to remind me of this when after hitting a long fly ball for an out he would wail "Where in hell do you ever find these lousy softballs." I discovered with time that Jim had a good point (though, like all of us, his slowly aging joints and muscles were possibly relevant as well). The only time it might be strategically wise to provide softballs that are cheap and "dead" is if your team is responsible for providing the balls for both teams and the other team has the substantial advantage in power hitting. Since in most leagues the balls used by a team are provided by that same team, I've come to agree with Jim that it's worthwhile for a team to put out some extra money and get a good lively ball (getting the team to cough up the required money, if they are not sponsored, is another task indeed).

While they were content to peck cautiously at the ball, he never spared himself in his efforts to do it violent injury.
P.G. Wodehouse
(1881–1975)
My Man Jeeves

Hitting for Power

The Duke of Windsor is purported to have said, "You can never be too thin or too rich." In softball, that adage, at least in regard to offense, might be changed to "you can never be too big or too rich."

To hit with power generally requires four basic steps: 1) the bat must be gripped very tightly so that whatever force that is exerted by the body is effectively transferred to the ball; 2) body weight must be transferred from the rear leg to the front leg, while upper body strength is exerted as the bat meets the ball; 3) the bat must make solid contact with the ball; and 4) there must be adequate follow-through after hitting the ball. In addition, *both* sheer body mass and muscle strength appear to be key factors in how far a softball can be hit.

Body mass is actually a more important factor in slow-pitch softball than in baseball or fast-pitch softball. This is because the *inertia* of the ball at the time it is struck by the bat is so much greater in slow-pitch softball; this is a result of both the slow pitch itself and low density of the ball used. Thus the foot-pounds of impact needed to propel the ball is greater, and body weight is a major factor in generating this impact over inertia.

The issue of both body mass and strength are especially relevant to the second basic step in hitting with power, which involves the transference of strength and sheer body mass into pounds of pressure applied to the ball as it is hit. Contrary to popular belief, body mass *alone* is not the only factor in hitting with power, though it is a definite, major factor. However, many players of great weight don't hit the ball very far, because they fail to properly transform their weight and power. This is either because they hit only with their upper body, or there is little transfer of weight from one foot to the other. Most softball players who hit for long distances are not only large, but are powerful and have strong wrists. It's this combination of bulk, strength, powerful wrists, and ability to move that bulk into the ball that allows them to hit for great distances.

Good size, or body mass, along with powerful muscle development make for a true power hitter, as is evidenced by Ronnie Jernigan of the Hickory Hammock team from Milton, Florida.
Photograph by Randy
Courtesy of ASA

95

Thus, any strategies designed to increase the distance that the ball is hit should emphasize making good contact and improving transference of body weight and strength into the swing. Exercises to increase the visual skills so necessary to good batting are detailed in the following section on playing the game better. Increasing one's body weight will do little good unless increased strength is associated with it. Weight training aimed at developing increased strength will provide the desired increases in both strength and weight, and it is also discussed in a later section of this book.

Greater love hath no man than this, that a man lend his bat to his teammates.
John XV. 13.

Bat Preference

Since bats come in a variety of shapes and sizes it is important that the batter feel comfortable with the bat being used and have confidence in it. The power delivered to the ball is directly proportional to the amount of kinetic energy delivered to it by the bat. This kinetic energy produced is directly proportional to the weight of the bat, and the *square* of the speed of the swing. Thus, an increase in the speed of the swing while keeping bat weight constant will produce a larger increase in power than a proportionately equal increase in bat weight while keeping the speed of the swing constant.

The key to making a proper bat selection, then, is in selecting the heaviest bat that will allow for a quick swing.

As regards aluminum bats versus wooden bats, there appears to be no significant difference in power delivered to the ball if the ball is struck squarely. However, there is some evidence that when the ball is struck on the upper or lower edges of the bat, an aluminum bat will deliver slightly more power to the ball. Many players favor wooden bats for the more solid sound or "click" given off when the ball is hit, and for the sense that they can "whip" it more effectively.

It's interesting that many players who use aluminum bats still carry the old habit (associated with the use of wooden bats) of having the trademark on the bat face upward as the bat is swung into the ball. This is because with a wooden bat the trademark is always on the "flat of the grain," which allows the ball to be hit with a more solid impact. Obviously, no such issue is in actuality associated with an aluminum bat.

It is also interesting to note the psychological factors associated with the use of a bat. Players become almost superstitious about their bats, and how many hits there are in it. I've seen this carried to the extreme where batters feel that they can only get hits with a certain type of a bat, and are reduced to quivering jelly if forced to use another bat for some reason. The issue of such confidence was dramatically exhibited in an incident with a player I played with over a number of years. Through one period he was using a bat that had the label "Sluggerette" embossed on it, apparently having been intended for use by women. He had used this bat with great succes over six games, when in the seventh game one of his teammates discovered the "Sluggerette" label. After this was quickly communicated to the rest of the players, a howl of kidding and derision toward this player followed. He manfully used the bat on his next two times at bat, but did not hit successfully in either attempt. This set off even more catcalls, both by his teammates and the other team, who by then had discovered what had happened. Not surprisingly, he stopped using the bat after this and did not hit as well during the rest of the season as he had in the six games prior.

To swing, or not to swing?
That is the question:
William Shakespeare
(1564-1616)
Hamlet

Bat Control

In addition to hitting with power, two general characteristics needed in order to be a good hitter are 1) the ability to hit the ball into a specific area, and 2) the ability to hit the ball in the direction optimally afforded by the placement of the pitch. The first necessitates being able to adjust the point during the swing at which the ball is hit. Because the face of the bat travels in an arc, a ball hit early in the swing will travel to the field opposite the side of home plate on which the batter is standing. For the same reason, a ball hit midway in the swing will travel to the middle of the field, and a ball hit late in the swing will be "pulled" to the field closest to the side of home plate on which the batter is standing.

Obviously, the chief way of controlling the point when the ball will be hit during the arc of the swing is to adjust the timing of the swing. By swinging earlier than usual, the bat meets the ball later in the arc of the bat, resulting in the ball being "pulled." Likewise, a swing that is slightly delayed will result in the bat meeting the ball in an early stage of the arc, thus driving it into the "opposite" field. In addition to adjusting the timing of their swing, many players also shift the position of their body in relation to the pitch so that the arc of the swing is also shifted. For example, by "closing" the batting stance, which means shifting the side of the body closest to the pitcher closer to the plate, the arc of the swing is adjusted so that even pitches hit late in the swing will travel to the opposite field. Conversely, by "opening" the batting stance, even pitches hit early in the swing will tend to be pulled.

97

While place hitting sounds fairly simple, it takes most players many hours of practice to learn how to adjust the timing of their swing without messing up such factors as the power of the swing, the level plane of the swing, etc. In addition, there is another complicating factor that must be taken into account: the placement of the pitch. As can be seen in the accompanying diagrams, the placement of the ball affects the trajectory of a hit ball. A ball on the outside of the plate can be difficult to "pull," just as an inside pitch can be difficult to hit to the opposite field. Either would require shifts in both the timing of the swing and the batting stance. A further complication is that with a well-placed pitch, there will only be a split second during which good contact can be made. Trying to hit it sooner or later in its flight would likely result in a poorly hit ball. While better players are quickly able to recognize the placement of a pitch, and simultaneously adjust their swing and stance in order to still hit the ball to a predetermined spot, many players are unable to do so on any consistent basis. Practice is critical to the development of this skill.

Still another complicating factor, however, is the importance of being able to place a hit toward a particular area when runners are on base (discussed below). In this case, the batter has the choice of 1) waiting for the optimal pitch, with the risk of getting behind in the count; 2) trying to place the ball to a predetermined spot regardless of where it is pitched, with the risk of hitting the ball poorly; or 3) going with the pitch, yet knowing that such ball placement may not be ideal for the given situation.

He's happy, who, far away from business like the race of men of old, plays softball.
    Horace
    (65-8 B.C.)
    Epodes

Placing the Hit

Place hitting, especially hitting to the opposite field, is a skill that every player should develop. Unfortunately, many softball players can only pull the ball. Players who can place the ball will be able to hit to open areas and to weak infielders or outfielders, thus gaining the advantage of not allowing the opposition to drift into a defensive shift into any one area.

Much of place hitting strategy depends on the presence or absence of runners on base, the positioning of the runners on base, and the number of outs. When there are no base runners, the choice of where to direct the hit depends on the individual preferences and skills of the batter. However, an argument can be made that right-handed batters should hit to the left side of the field. First of all, a right-handed batter will be able to hit the ball with more power to the left side. Secondly, the fielders on the left side have a longer throw to make to first base, and if the ball is bobbled it's much more likely the batter can beat the throw. I personally favor specifically hitting to the third baseman with nobody on, again for two reasons. As a right-handed batter, the maximum power can be delivered to a ball hit toward the third base area, increasing the chances of the ball going through, or being bobbled for an error. Secondly, of the two fielders on the left side, the third baseman is almost always the weaker fielder, again increasing the chances of getting on base.

For left handers, I would favor pulling the ball to the first baseman. Again, the first baseman is usually the weaker of the two infielders on the right side, and when a ball is bobbled by the first baseman, most softball teams have not worked out a very smooth play for the pitcher to cover first.

With the exception of power hitters or a situation calling for a sacrifice fly, any hits with runners on base should be line drives or grounders, rather than fly balls. Keeping the ball down increases the chance of the ball being mishandled and offers more chances for runners to advance.

If there are single runners on base (first, second, or third base only) and less than two outs, the primary duty of the batter is to advance the runner. If the runner is on third, the ball should be hit out of the infield with power so that at the very least the runner can score by tagging up. If runners are on first or second, the ball should be hit to the right side of the field. This is because a ball hit safely to the right side increases the likelihood of a runner on first being able to advance to third due to the longer throw required to third. And a ball hit to the right side with a runner on second, even if only a grounder, usually allows the runner to advance to third, because of the long secondary throw to third.

When more than one runner is on base with less than two outs, the ball should again be hit to the right side of the field, basically for the same advantage noted above. The one exception might be when one of the runners is on third base, and the top priority is getting that run in. In that case, hitting out of the infield with power, to whatever field, would be the desired strategy.

When runners are on base with two outs, batting strategy naturally changes. It would do little good to advance a runner at the expense of an out if it's the third out. A two-out situation thus calls for the batter to use whatever strategy is needed to maximize getting a hit, regardless of the directon.

As is undoubtedly evident from the above discussion, it is essential that softball players be able to hit with power and consistency to right field. This is one of the reasons for the maxim "bat left; throw right" (the other being the fact that the left-handed hitter is two steps closer to first base every time he or she is up to bat during a career; that can be many,

many steps saved overall). Unfortunately, the majority of softball players, even in advanced skill leagues, have not developed much consistency or power to right field. This seriously weakens their ability to handle some of the strategic situations mentioned above. The reasons for not being able to hit to right field are either a lack of practice in developing this skill or an exaggerated commitment by right handers to a batting style that emphasizes pulling the ball directly down the line. Practice, and a challenging of that belief by coaches and teammates are the antidotes, respectively. With enough practice, players can even learn to shift their feet as they swing, as opposed to when they first set up in the batter's box. This prevents defensive players from quickly recognizing an attempt to hit to right field.

***I could not love thee, dear, so much
loved I not softball more.***
Sir Richard Lovelace
(1618-1658)
*To Lucasta on Going
to the Wars*

Changing Batting Styles

One problem seen in many aging softball players is their unwillingness to adapt their batting style to reduced physical skills. It's a simple fact that as we age we lose reflex speed and muscle strength. Unfortunately, many aging players spend a couple of years looking for the old days of glory. Though they swing with all the power they can muster, it now just isn't enough. Such players unfortunately often delay developing the skill to place their hits (even with power) to the opposite field, and thus can become a real liability to a team. The wise player has developed these skills before the power starts to go.

A change in batting style may also be dictated by the types of pitches being thrown, or by the type of pitches the umpire is accepting as strikes. Assessing this is an important task for the batters early in the line up, and for the coaches. They should try to look for any inconsistent patterns here, such as allowing balls that are below six feet to be called strikes, allowing extra high pitches to be called strikes, inside or outside pitches being more readily accepted as strikes, etc. This information can be used in two ways. First, it is worthwhile to communicate it to all the other batters on the team so that they can be prepared accordingly, possibly shifting their batting stance either away or closer to the plate or short or deep in the batting box to account for this.

Secondly, it may be worthwhile to give feedback (with some diplomacy) to the umpires. Umpires who accept too many flat pitches, for example, will often retract from this position if they are hassled by coaches. A team should consider, however, whether they want the umpire to change this decision process. Though he or she may be calling off-the-plate pitches as strikes, and certain well placed pitches as balls, this may be to the advantage of the team, given their particular hitting style and the opposition's hitting style. This should at least be considered before immediately jumping on the umpire for "bad calls."

Errors like straws upon the surface flow.
He who would search for hits must hit low.
    John Dryden
    (1631-1700)
    All for Love (Prologue)

Batting Faults

There are a number of faults commonly seen in various batters. The major one is not getting the whole body into the swing. A great many players swing only from the waist up, keeping the lower torso relatively immobile. I had a good friend that I played with for years who had this fault. Almost every time that he came to bat we advised him to swing with his whole body, and he just could not, or would not, do so. He was a powerful looking man and yet seldom hit the ball even as far as the standard outfield position. Of course, in the early parts of a season he was able to get a few hits by having his longest hits drop in safely. But with just a little time others in the league became aware of this, and quickly reduced his offensive effectiveness to a low level.

A second mistake that batters make is to undercut the ball, what is referred to as a "golf swing." It is tempting to do this since it seems as if one could power the ball over the outfielders' heads with such a swing. However, more often than not the ball will just become a high fly ball, even when it is hit with substantial force. The ideal swing is one that cuts straight through the ball and remains level throughout. This results in line drives, the most effective type of hit in softball. Unless one has massive power, one should always be trying to hit line drives. An ideal goal is to try to hit the ball such that it is a hard line drive that will hit at the front part of the infield. If it is hit hard, it is likely to go through the holes in the infield. In the few areas that can be covered by an infielder, the short hop makes it a very difficult play.

Many players also make a mistake of taking too long of a stride into the ball. This does not actually increase power, and in fact, may reduce it as it is very easy to lose balance. Also, the long stride reduces the speed with which one can make the break to first base.

Another major fault is to ignore or forget that a base on balls is often as good as a hit. The only time this would not be a fault is in a game situation where a powerful batter is up with runners on second and/or third, a

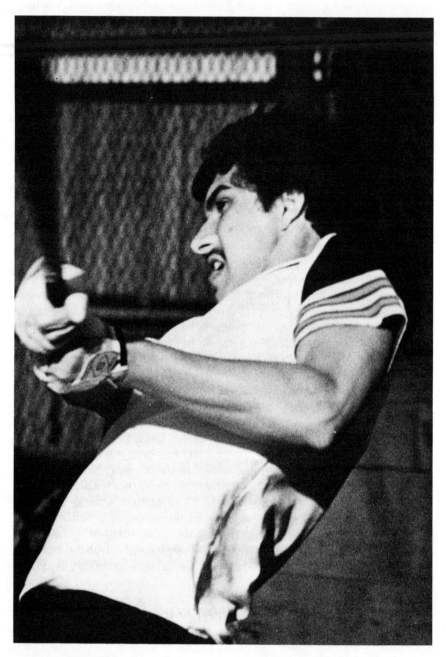

A second mistake that batters make is to undercut the ball.

relatively weak batter is coming up next, and there are two outs. If the batter walks in a situation like that, there is little gain (unless the team is several runs down in the last inning), since the risk is high that the relatively weak hitter will not deliver the needed hit. Of course, alert opponents that do their homework with a little scouting wisely and purposely walk batters in such instances.

A related fault is that many players are too overeager to hit against a pitcher who is having difficulty getting the ball over the plate. If a pitcher has been giving out walks with any regularity at all, it's wise to take a few pitches (at least taking one strike) in order to force the pitcher to come in with a good pitch. I've seen many a game in which a pitcher who is having control problems delivers two or three balls and then the batter swings on the next pitch, only to become an out. This is very poor judgement, as the statistical likelihood of getting on base with a base on balls in such a situation is high.

Many players new to softball make the mistake of trying to bunt or trying to swing very slowly on a pitch, which is then usually interpreted by the umpire as a bunt. The bunt is illegal in slow-pitch softball (though not in fast-pitch softball) and new players should be aware of this from the start, usually through good coaching.

Another fault is not staying aware of the foul and out rule. In some leagues the batter may be allowed to foul off two balls after two strikes and only be called out on the third foul ball after that. However, in a number of other leagues any foul balls after two strikes result in an out. I have seen numerous players get to two strikes, foul off the next one, be called out, and then protest vehemently about this foul and out rule. The problem is that they just weren't aware of the rule, had not asked ahead of time, and now look a little silly. Of course, a good coach covers this before the game so that everyone knows the foul and out rule ahead of time.

Finally, a really embarrassing mistake is to take a called third strike. Whenever batters have two strikes on them, they are advised to swing at any close pitches. Most slow-pitch softball umpires seldom get to call a third strike, and often seem to take a perverse delight in doing so. Thus, batters should be prepared to hit any pitch reasonably close to the strike zone if two strikes have already been tallied. It is for this reason that players should practice hitting balls that are not exactly down the center of the plate.

Where there is only one more out to go, there's hope, he cried.

John Gay
(1685-1732)
*The Sick Man and
the Angel*

Batting Order

The order in which players bat will play a significant role in a team's offensive success or failure, due to the advantages inherent in having particularly skilled batters up in various situations.

Lead Off Batter—The lead off batter should be the player who will be on base most often over the whole season, whether through hits, walks, beating out close plays, etc. This batter should also possess good speed and be a "heads up" base runner, as the primary task of batters that follow will be to advance this runner. The lead off batter should seldom hit a fly ball.

Second Batter—The second batter should also hit for a good average and consistently get on base. In addition, he or she should possess the ability to advance runners by being able to hit the ball to the right side of the field with power and placement. Since it is important that this batter be quick enough to get to first base in order to avoid any double plays, this is a good spot to bat a left-handed batter who is a competent hitter. As noted earlier, the left-handed batter is already two steps closer to first base and will naturally be more able to consistently hit the ball with power to right field.

Third Batter—The third batter in the line-up should be the player on the team with the best combination of power and consistency. This is also a good spot for a left-handed batter because the third batter also often needs to avoid double plays. It is also helpful if he or she can hit with power to the right side and can deliver the long fly ball when needed to bring in a single critical run.

Dick Bartel of San Antonio, Texas is an ideal cleanup hitter, having won the ASA National Home Run Contest in Oklahoma City.
Photo courtesy of ASA

Clean up Hitter (Number 4 batter)—The clean up hitter should be able to deliver the home run ball, or at least hit consistently with power. I have, however, found that a number of players don't like to bat in the number 4 position, even though they have tremendous power, because the expectancy placed upon them to deliver big hits disrupts their performance. Thus, an awareness of the psychological preferences and attitudes of the various players helps in putting together a good batting order.

Fifth Batter—The number 5 batter should be able to deliver the ball with power to all fields; not only because runners will often be on the bases, but because it prevents the opposing pitcher from pitching around the number 4 batter. If there is a weak batter in the number 5 position, the number 4 batter will either get very bad pitches or be walked intentionally.

Numbers Six, Seven, and Eight Batters—These batters are not as strong as the preceeding batters in any of the skills mentioned, though they are not as weak as the 9th and 10th batters usually are. On a team of average or weaker players, I tend to simply bat hitters 6 through 8 in order of ability, the 6th batter being the strongest and 8th being the weakest. When a team has solid hitting throughout most of the lineup, I then bat persons who get on base more consistently in the 6th and 7th spot and reserve the 8th spot for a power hitter.

Ninth Batter—There are diverse opinions among coaches as to whether the weakest hitter on a team should bat 9th or 10th. My own preference is to bat the weakest hitter in the 9th spot on many occasions, especially if my team is average or below average in overall ability. On a team with good hitters throughout the lineup, I bat the weakest hitter at the number 10 spot. Experience with a particular set of teammates is very helpful here. I have found some players who react very poorly to batting in the number 10 spot, taking it as an insult. For others it is a "liberation," because any hits they get are better than what was implicitly expected of them. Speed on the bases is another consideration in determining these positions. Fast players should not be slowed by having very slow players in front of them. Consequently, I prefer to put a weak hitter who is fast in the 10th spot in order not to slow up the lead off hitter.

Teams in the intermediate and lower skill levels of softball competition often have a "hole" in the batting order, a series of weak hitters, usually in the sixth through tenth batting positions. It's true that sometimes this hole is unavoidable, simply dictated by the player selection and availability. The problem is compounded by the fact that many of these players do not have much "softball sense" that could lessen some of the harm that they might do to a rally and to the offense in general. For example, people in the "hole" should be alert toward any possibility of getting on base via a walk. They should also take extra practice on hitting to right field so that at least they can advance the runners, even if they are unlikely to make a powerful hit. They should also be coached on the recognition of the weak spots in the other team's defense, and then to make every effort to hit to those weak spots. By using these coping strategies, there can be at least a minimal contribution from this part of the order, allowing the overall offense to function more adequately.

The task of developing an effective batting order belongs to the coach, the subject of the last subsection of this overall section on how to play the game. Before discussing coaching, however, we'll consider another major aspect of the offense, baserunning.

Dost thou love life, then do not squander chances to play softball, for that is the stuff life is made of.
Benjamin Franklin
(1706-1790)
Poor Richard

Base Running

**A fleet foot is
a great gift of nature.**
Johann Wolfgang Von Goethe
(1742-1832)
Elective Affinities

Techniques

Base running is a most important skill in softball, yet the development of this skill is often ignored by coaches and players alike. While the actual running of bases theoretically can be practiced, most people who are beyond that psychotic phase of development termed adolescence feel a little silly running around sliding into bases on an empty softball field. A more reasonable and appropriate approach to better base running emphasizes improvement in physical conditioning, running strategy, and possibly the practice of base running by Imagery Rehearsal (described in the next overall section of this book on Playing the Game Better).

Running speed is obviously the essential physical requirement involved in base running. Conditioning of the legs and the cardio-pulmonary system through sprints can help a player improve running speed. Yet, the extent of improvement will naturally depend to a substantial degree upon natural endowment. Nevertheless, a training emphasis should not be focused only on increasing speed, since *stamina* plays an important role in maintaining maximum running speed potential throughout a game. In this regard, running sprints, both before and after practice, can be helpful, as can the periodic running of longer distances at a slower pace.

Speed on the bases can also be improved by certain running techniques. For example, as runners near a base, they should begin a modest rounding approach. This allows a runner to step on the inside corner of the base and push off toward the next base. Such a turn reduces the amount of ground to be covered by decreasing the angle of the turn, and also allows the player to continue to the next base without breaking stride.

Even when a runner is unlikely to be able to advance further, such a turn should be made to allow for continued advancement if an unexpected opportunity develops as a result of play in the field. Obviously, any significant turn would not be desirable when the ball is close by.

The exceptions to this base running strategy would be when a batter is advancing to first base on a close play, when a runner is advancing to home plate, or when a slide is required to reach base safely. Since the runner is allowed to overrun first base, and since no further advance-

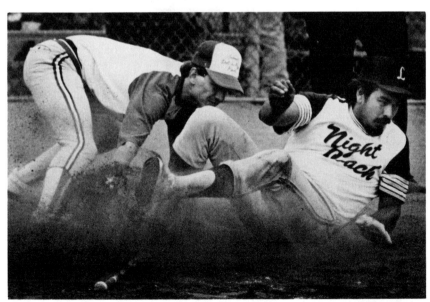

Base running is a critical skill in softball, yet the development of this skill is often ignored by coaches and players alike.

Running speed is obviously the essential physical requirement involved in base running.

ment is likely following a close play, the fastest route to first base on a close play is straight through the base. Similarly, in a play close enough to require a slide, a straight-in approach is again the fastest route. In an advance to home plate, it obviously isn't possible to go on to another base, so the faster straight-in approach is used.

The starting position of the base runner already on base is also important to base running speed. Most players use the traditional *baseball stance* wherein the player stands to the advancing side of the base facing the pitcher's mound, with the trailing left foot in a position to push off the side of the base. The feet are bent slightly, and are spread more than shoulders' length apart, with the knees bent slightly. While such a stance is used in baseball mainly to allow a player to watch a pitcher, and to keep from being picked off, there is no such worry in slow pitch softball since runners aren't allowed to leave the base until the ball is hit. However, such a stance does allow the advantage of a quick lateral movement which is of key importance if there is a need to return to the original base just after having already started toward the next base. This is most often necessary in the case of a fielded line drive. By starting out in a sideways position with respect to the next base, a runner can laterally shuffle the first couple of steps and still be in a position to return quickly to the original base with a similar shuffling movement.

This is not true, however, for the most common alternative stance employed, the *track stance*. This stance is somewhat similar to the starting position of a track and field sprinter, with the base runner's body facing the next base. The knees are again bent, with the trailing foot in a position to push off from the side of the base. In this case, the head must sometimes be bent slightly to see the pitcher-batter exchange. The obvious advantage to this stance is that all running energy is spent in moving directly toward the next base. Rather than having to spend time and energy after the first several steps in squaring up the body toward the next base, only the head needs to be straightened. We're talking here in terms of only a second or so saved, but the outcome of many plays is decided by split-seconds.

The disadvantage of such a stance, however, is that in order to return to a base, the body has to be turned approximately 90 degrees so that one can best move laterally back to the base. In the case of a "bang-bang" play like a caught line drive, the time it takes to spin could prove to be critical.

Given the advantages and disadvantages of both stances, the reasonable base running strategy would be to employ the style that is most efficient in a particular situation. If a runner is on base with less than two outs, the possibility of a caught line drive doubling the runner off base suggests the use of the traditional baseball stance. However, if a runner is on base in a "must run" situation with two outs, it is irrelevant to worry about being "doubled up," and the track stance is suggested.

The track stance is favored by most baserunners in slow-pitch softball, as it allows a quick start on the ball.
Photo by Paul Salmon

Similarly, when tagging up on a caught fly ball, a runner already at the base does not need to worry about getting back, and should use the track stance.

Specific Strategies
While running speed is critical to being an excellent base runner, players with average or even less than average speed can be adequate base runners if they use good strategy. This requires knowing what to do in any situation and then using good judgment as the play breaks.

Probably the most crucial element in good base running strategy is deciding whether to begin advancing to the next base or not. This involves 1) being able to accurately decide whether your base running abilities will allow you to reach the next base safely, and 2) recognizing those situations in which the rules of the game mandate that you attempt to advance to the next base (a "force play").

Much of the task of deciding whether or not a player can make it to the next base is the responsibility of the base coaches, a task discussed in some detail later in this section. While this is particularly true of teams in the better leagues, it has been my experience that base coaches in leagues of a lesser caliber occasionally hurt runners more than help them. This can be due to an 1) unfamiliarity with their teammates' running skills, 2) ignorance of good base running strategy, and/or 3) just plain poor judgment. For whatever reason, then, it is important that players know their own base running abilities and limitations, and be prepared to occasionally override a coach's base running directions.

Audentis Fortuna iuvat
Fortune assists the bold
Virgil
(70-19 B.C.)
Aeneid

Running From Base to Base
When a runner is on any of the bases with two outs, they should leave the base the instant the ball is hit, and from that point on simply pay attention to the play as they can see it, and to the directions from the coaches. No matter how many outs, the runner on first base should strongly consider going to third base on any safe hit into right field. Depending on the arms of the other outfielders, it is probably wise to challenge them early in the game. Making an out by throwing to a base to tag a runner out demands, 1) a good fielding play by the outfielder, 2) a quick and accurate throw to the person covering the base or to the relay person, 3) accurate catches on all throws, and 4) a well placed tag in time to beat the runner. There are many points in this sequence where error can occur. Even if the runner is tagged out at third base, it's likely the move to third base brought the batter down to second, so the cost is not terribly high given the potential overall benefits.

Runners should be especially aware of the position and reactions of any runners behind them on the other bases. The lead runner may have to run on a ground ball to avoid setting up an easy double play, or in rare instances, a triple play.

When there is a runner on second base and no one on first base, and less than two outs, the runner should usually hold on a grounder hit to the left side of the infield, but advance to third base if the ground ball is hit to the right side. Even on balls hit to the left side, a fast runner may occasionally immediately break for third as the shortstop or third baseman releases the ball to first, and then pay close attention to the third base coach for a signal to slide or stand up.

When a runner is on third base and there are less than two outs and no one on second base and first, that runner should stay close to third on any ground ball hit to the third baseman. As the ball is thrown by the third baseman to first, the runner can make the break, depending on his speed and his estimate of the catcher's general ability, realizing that catchers are relatively weak fielders. In intermediate and lower level softball leagues, they are reasonably likely to make an error, either physical or mental, in a close situation such as this. This strategy is most useful if one's team is ahead, as this will pad the lead, or if one's team is fairly far behind, since this may ignite the morale of the team and possibly disrupt the confidence of the other team. When one run is crucial, the runner is advised to always hold at third base if there are one out or no outs, since it's quite probable that he or she will be able to score later on.

Awareness of whether or not advancement to the next base is necessary is also important. If a runner is on base, and there is no open base between the runner and the batter, it's already been noted that the runner must try to advance to the next base if a batted ball touches the ground. If a batted ball is caught on the fly, runners don't have to advance, and can potentially be tagged out for advancing off a base before the ball is caught. Thus, a runner on base with less than two outs must be ready for a number of situations. If there are no open bases between the runner and batter, the runner must be able to quickly decide whether a batted ball is going to touch the ground or not. If it is, a quick start is essential to keep from being thrown out. If it is not, the runner must be close enough to the base to keep from being picked off.

In the case of sharp line drives to the infield, this decision must be immediate. Watching the trajectory of the ball as it leaves the bat is critical, as is the strategy of waiting until the ball clears the infield before advancing to the next base.

Balls hit to the outfield in such a situation require that a runner move to a position "halfway" to the next base. In this way, if the ball is not caught the runner can advance safely to the next base, while if it is caught the runner can safety return. In either case, only half of the base path need be covered.

Though the "halfway" strategy with less than two outs is pretty much a commonly accepted rule, it has been my experience that with the short base paths in softball, the faster runners can often employ a "tag up' strategy here. This is particularly true for balls hit deep that are obviously catchable. By employing a "tag up" strategy, faster runners are able to still advance a base even on a caught ball, while their speed still allows them to safely reach the next base if the ball happens to fall in for a hit or is dropped.

A second string right fielder galloping after a sinking line drive—The unskilled in full pursuit of the uncatchable.
Oscar Wilde
(1854-1900)
A Woman of No Importance

General Strategies

While there are some standard general base running strategies, these must often be adjusted from game to game, depending mainly upon both one's own personnel and the abilities of the opponent. It is usually a good idea to be very aggressive (take chances) early in the game, and for two reasons. First, this helps to identify the fielding and throwing abilities of the opposing outfielders. This information can then be used to gauge later hitting and base running strategies.

In one game that I managed, aggressive base running in the early innings allowed us to discover that the other team's right center fielder had an injured throwing arm and had to always throw to a short relay man to even get the ball in. We capitalized on this periodically throughout the game. But we did not try to run it into the ground since we were a couple of runs ahead and did not want him replaced by someone with a much stronger arm, even though that might have given them a bit less offense. In the last inning we had fallen behind by one run. Since he could hardly even throw at all by this point, any ball hit to him was virtually an automatic double and base runners could easily take two bases. As a result, a purposeful succession of hits to this right center fielder led to a quick rally that won the game.

A second and related advantage of aggressive base running is that it may disrupt the general concentration of outfielders, therefore causing subsequent errors on fly balls and hard grounders. The biggest mistakes that outfielders can make is to start focusing on the throw and making anticipatory movements well before they have actually fielded the ball effectively. Aggressive base running can start this negative cycle.

Runners who are tagging up on a fly ball should, of course, make sure that they do not leave the base too early. The best technique is to give either the first or third base coach the responsibility to call out when the ball is caught. This way the runner can lean forward in the track stance and concentrate entirely on getting a good start. Runners coming into any base other than home plate should attend to the coach's instructions whether to move on. If they are coming into home base, they should be coached as to whether they need to slide or stand up. Usually the lead runner or the person next up to bat will take this responsibility. The coach should be aware of the possibilities here, and may need to directly take over this role.

If base runners get caught off base, it is their responsibility to "stay alive" (avoid being tagged) as long as possible. By staying alive in a "rundown," the runner allows other base runners to advance as far as possible, so that at least some good can be salvaged out of the situation. There is also an increasing chance that an error will occur the longer the rundown goes on.

Some runners will even try to aggressively slide into first base to beat a close throw. The only type of slide which saves any real time here is a headfirst slide, and this has to be executed perfectly to save even a split second. Since the potential for injury to a player is relatively high in a head first slide, the cost-benefit ratio of gaining that split second is negative when it's realized that a valuable player can be lost for the game if not for the season, not to mention the probable physical damage to the player. Thus it is recommended that one never slide into first base unless it is necessary to quickly dodge an attempted tag by a first baseman who has been pulled off the base by an infielder's throw.

I only regret that
I have but one life
to give to softball. . .
Nathan Hale
(1755-1776)
Speech before his execution
as a spy by the British

Sliding

An important complement to good base running skills is the ability to execute an effective slide into a base on a close play. There are three basic slides: 1) The straight-in slide; 2) the hook slide; and 3) the head first slide. Novices at sliding should receive direct supervision from a good coach before trying any of these slides.

The straight-in and hook slides are the more traditional methods of sliding and are similar in a number of ways. Both involve sliding feet-first into the base, with contact (the "tagging" of the base) made with one of the feet. In each case, as the base is approached, the runner shifts into a "reclined sitting position." The hips are turned so that one or the other of the legs is tucked up and under to bear the brunt of the slide. This "sliding leg" is somewhat bent, with body weight distributed such that the friction of the slide is evenly distributed down the leg from the hip to the knee. The arms are kept up in the air in order to maintain balance.

The differences between these two sliding styles are related to the various purposes each is optimal for. The straight-in slide is the quicker of the two, and is generally used when runners feel that such a slide will enable them to beat a throw to the base. The slide is made straight into the base, with the tag of the base made by the non-sliding leg, which is extended relatively straight out in front of the body.

The hook slide, on the other hand, is used mainly to avoid a tag, so it is employed when it appears that the ball will arrive with or before the runner. Since fielders usually set up to receive a throw on the side of the base closest to the origin of the throw, the approach for a hook slide is toward the side *opposite* the throw. Rather than sliding *into* the base, the runner will aim to slide *by* the base. This slide gets its name from the manner in which the base is then "hooked" (or tagged) by the foot. The non-sliding leg is again used to tag the base, but in this case this leg is bent out in the direction of the base so that it, in effect, is "hooked" as the runner slides by. By hook sliding to the side opposite the throw, the runner forces the fielder to provide the necessary extra time required to touch the base safely.

If you don't go after things in this world You don't get things.
President Ronald Reagan
In the movie *Kings Row*

The head first slide is similar to the straight-in slide in that the actual slide is aimed directly at the base. In this case, however, the slide consists of a diving motion toward the base. The brunt of the slide is absorbed by the chest and stomach, and the base is touched by the outstretched hands. Most experts feel that this is the fastest of the three slides, based on body motion and momentum.

Good sprinting form dictates that the body be leaning slightly forward when this slide is initiated. A head first slide is a reasonably natural extension of this forward lean in terms of both momentum and motion. The forward, driving motion fo the legs, for example, can be used to naturally spring the body forward into a diving position. On the other hand, the more traditional feet first slides require that the natural stride of the runner stop as the lower body is swiveled forward. The momentum of the upper body also shifts from a forward to a backward lean in the feet first slides.

However, many coaches and players feel that the extra speed afforded by the head first slide is offset by an increased risk of injury. The most common injuries involve the hands and wrists, ranging from sprains and cuts to broken bones. The face, head, and neck are also quite vulnerable to injury inflicted by the base covering defensive player.

The head first slide is effective, but as you can see, also risky (and dusty).
Photo by Chuck DeLoach
Courtesy of the Clearwater
Sun and ASA

The injuries commonly generated by all three types of slides are primarily related to the timing of the slide. Slides that are begun too late result in too much momentum being carried into the base and the defensive player. This may lead to oversliding the base and subsequently being tagged out, or more importantly, a very dangerous jarring of the body as it smashes into the base. The key here, of course, is for runners to gradually and incrementally practice and learn where to begin their slide so that they have just enough momentum to carry them quickly into the base.

As in all other phases of the game, practice is important here. Yet, most amateur softball players almost never practice slides. But when it has been practiced, well-learned, and is then well-executed, it is a thing of beauty. An outfielder on a number of teams I have played with, and a fellow who helped out a great deal on this book, Mile Moll, was very adept at the straight-in slide, usually popping up as if he had a spring under him. He gained many an extra base because of this slide since whenever the ball went through the tag, he was always ready to move on to the next base.

In summary, then, the ability to execute a proper slide can be very advantageous to a player's base running. However, this aspect of the game holds a high potential for injury if not properly executed. Thus, players might want to evaluate whether their abilities, age, or the level of competition in a game warrant its use. Older players especially run a risk of injury when sliding, and coaches should be aware of this as they respond to their individual players. It is, after all, just a game, and the risk of an injury that could linger on for many years simply isn't worth the cost, especially if a player is older or is not skilled in sliding.

I am ashes where once I was fire.
Lord Byron
(1788-1824)
To the Countess of Blessington

Coaching-Managing

Go call a coach,
and let a coach be called . . .
But Coach! Coach! Coach!
Oh for a coach, Ye gods!
> Henry Carey
> (1693-1743)
> *Chrononhotonthologos*

The Coach

Technically, the manager is the person in overall charge of the team, and the coach is a type of assistant (possibly a role shared by team members on a revolving basis). In actual practice, the distinction between "manager" and "coach" blurs, and we will talk about their respective functions under the one term "coaching" in both this section and in the book in general.

The coach or manager always has some basic things to do in softball games, such as making sure enough people show up for the game, writing up the line up, and bringing the balls. When the team is a good team and has played together for some time, there may be only a few other tasks. The job gets more and more complex to the degree either of these two conditions are not fulfilled.

That complexity centers on generating and keeping the team playing well, communicating well, and playing with a positive tempo and morale. All of the instructions, advice, and suggestions, that are laced throughout this book can be used by coaches to deal with "deficiencies" in their players, so in that broad sense this is a book on coaching. When working with players just breaking into the game, and especially if they have not had much prior experience with team and/or "ball" sports, virtually all of the material herein can be relevant. Fortunately, in most cases a coach will only have to use bits and pieces.

If coaches are going to take on the role of instructor, this should be an up-front contract with the player and/or team, especially if the focus is ever to be on basics. Most player expect a "laissez faire" (making very few decisions, and allowing team members virtual free rein) coach who does very little actual instructing. Thus, when such a coach does attempt some actual teaching, it may be seen as insulting by the player. Also, it is best to restrict such lessons to practices, or to messages communicated rather privately during an actual game. Publicly delivered instruction during a game has the taint of humiliation for most players receiving it, and this can only be negative for team morale. When dealing with someone who needs an overall perspective on softball, including some attention to basics, I recommend you have them obtain a good book on softball (modesty prevents me from strongly suggesting that you might recommend this book—at retail price, of course).

Every loss in a softball game
gives a foretaste of death;
every win a foretaste
of the resurrection ...
    Arthur Schopenhauer
    (1788-1860)
    Studies in Pessimism:
    Psychological Observations

Coaching Philosophy

Coaches can have an effect on the game through the philosophy they verbalize or demonstrate in practice. Coaches may differ on several relevant dimensions, such as whether they believe in winning-at-all costs, whether they prefer a conservative style of play, or whether they prefer a laissez-faire coaching style. These several dimensions are often interrelated. A laissez-faire coach is not likely to be constantly oriented toward winning at all costs. Nevertheless, these are dimensions that can be balanced in the approach of any one coach.

Reflecting the high emphasis placed on achievement and winning in our society, many coaches adopt a win-at-all costs philosophy. Unfortunately, this takes a lot of the fun out of the game. Only one team can win the final championship, but every team can have fun if they don't *need* to win it all. Teams that need to win at all costs are usually not peopled by players who are enjoying themselves. In fact, they appear to have some of the traits of addicts—a grim single-mindedness in pursuit of the goal, a willingness to ignore the rules or the feelings of others in order to attain victory, and a disruption of other phases of their lives, such as relations with loved ones and/or jobs. They can become chained to the supreme irony manifest in the Super Bowl or World Series winners who in the post-game interview wonder whether or not they will be able to win it all again next year.

Coaches who have a win-at-all costs philosophy usually are dominating in their approach to players. They are inclined to overinstruct, to play only the best players (except in games that are no longer really being contested), and to value seriousness and intensity over fun. The laissez-faire coach on the other hand may err by being too laid-back, allowing disorganization and inconsistency to develop. As in many situations in life, moderation appears to be the wise course here.

During the game itself, a coach makes choices that vary in degree of conservatism (see the prior section in this book on base running and coaching the bases). From an overall perspective, coaches will dictate whether a team is inclined to take chances and do the unexpected or perform in a more conservative and predictable fashion. The team that does the unexpected is more likely to disrupt the tempo of the opposition's play and thus gain an advantage. On the other hand, the conservative team is more likely to be consistent in their own play, and predictability does result in fewer errors in teamwork-dependent defensive plays and in base running.

He who overlooks an error promotes good will.
Book of Proverbs
Old Testament

The "First" Rule

Regardless of the coach's individual philosophy, the slogan "First pitch, first batter, first base" is worthwhile in most softball situations. "First pitch" refers to the importance of getting the first pitch in for a strike, as is noted earlier in the section on the pitcher. Many batters are reluctant to swing at the first pitch, or else are over eager to swing at it. In either case, a first pitch in the strike zone is invaluable.

The "first batter" refers to the importance of the first batter in an inning getting on base. The converse, of course, is that it is important for the defense to get the first batter out in each inning. Statistically, many more runs are scored when the first batter makes it to base. Thus, it is important to coach the skills for just getting on base, namely, taking pitches to increase the chance of a walk, place-hitting to take advantage of a weak fielder, and so on. This holds true even for power hitters, as they may occasionally lead off an inning. When players just get on first base in softball with no outs, it is highly probable that they will be able eventually to score.

The "first base" part of the maxim refers to the critical importance of keeping the lead runner restricted to first base as much as possible, and keeping any base runners from advancing to second base. The critical mistake made by most softball teams is not adopting a clear philosophy and plan for keeping runners off second base. Their major misjudgment is in making risky throws (usually inaccurately), or throwing to the wrong base. Even when a runner is continuing on from third to home, it is more worthwhile to throw to second to keep the hitter restricted to first base, unless it is an absolutely sure out at home. This issue is compounded by the fact that on many lesser skilled teams the catcher may be a weak player. Thus, the probabilities of getting the runner out at home may not be extremely high, even in the event of an accurate and timely throw. Conversely, so many outs are made on force plays, especially by teams of modest skills, that if the rule of keeping the lead runner on first is followed, the chance of winning is heightened immeasurably. This approach is the best prevention against big rallies, the time when that most important player, Mo Mentum, is likely to go over to the other side.

Still nursing the unconquerable hope. . .
Matthew Arnold
(1822-1872)
The Scholar Gypsy

Mo Mentum
For many years Don Meredith, the color commentator for ABC's Monday Night Football program, has pointed out how important it is to have that extra player, Mo Mentum, on one's team, and how Mo tends to switch sides at various times throughout the game. For example, momentum may subtly change sides if one team develops a big lead early in the game. From my own analysis of scoring patterns in various games, I find that it is much more worthwhile for a team to score one or more runs throughout several innings than to bunch the same number of runs in one or two innings. Concentration easily diminishes in the latter situation.

The real difficulty here is that it is hard to retain Mo Mentum's allegiance to your side once it has begun to slip away. Sometimes judicious substitution or a quick team meeting in which the coach reminds the team of what is happening to them can turn the process around, or at least halt it from continuing.

When Mo Mentum is on your side, an occasional great catch like this can happen.
Photo courtesy of ASA

Another situation that curbs a team's momentum is any drop-off in aggressive base running by that team. In many intances when a team has a big lead, their base runners stop trying for the extra base, and thus stop forcing outfielders to make difficult or challenging throws. As a result, the other team begins to feel more adequate in their fielding, and this usually carries over to their batting. As they gain any degree of success, they begin to have even more confidence, the cycle swings their way, and Mo Mentum, fickle as ever, changes sides again.

Never on the softball field
was so much owed
by so many to so few. . .
    Winston Churchill
    (1874-1965)
    Speech of 20 Aug. 1940

Coaching the Bases

The good base coach is someone who 1) can keep morale up with a line of chatter (without becoming too obnoxious even to one's own team), and yet at the same time 2) has a lot of experience with the game, 3) knows the important rules, and 4) has a good sense of how to capitalize on the weaknesses and strengths of the other team. Many a close softball game has been won or lost because of good base coaching. In that regard, scouting and/or observation of the other team is important in order to assess the strength and accuracy of the arm on each of their outfielders (and the infielders who make the relay throws).

Most softball teams don't pay much attention to who is coaching at first and third base. The job generally goes to people who are extra players, or else it is taken over by someone far down in the batting order from the person presently batting. This is fine in some respects, as it does give those extra players a sense of participating in the team venture. On the other hand, many of these players are less experienced and have less "softball sense" than the regulars on the team. For that reason, at least in close situations or in a critical game, a coach is wise to delegate these specific responsibilities to experienced players who have previously shown an ability to coach effectively. The most experienced person should take the third base coaching duties, since this involves the most responsibility and the trickiest decisions.

The first base coach really has only a few strategy responsibilities. The major ones are 1) whether the batter going to first base should run full tilt to beat the throw or begin to make the turn to go to second base and 2) when there is a runner on first base; whether that player a) knows the number of outs, is b) aware of the duty to try to break up any double play attempt, and c) is reminded of the probable need to go to third on any hit

Base coaches need to be alert and calculating.

into right field. The first base coach can also participate in making sure that a runner on second base knows the number of outs, though the third base coach has this as a primary responsibility.

The third base coach has to decide whether the runner needs to continue on from second base. In that sense he can override the first base coach's advice to go on to third on a hit to right field. The third base coach is really the one who controls the tempo of the base running. For example, the one time that aggressive base running is inexcusable is when the team is behind by a number of runs in the last inning. Lead base runners should be extremely conservative since they can only score if the runner behind them scores. Their runs mean nothing without the next runner eventually scoring.

Third base coaches also have the responsibility for telling runners whether or not they are to slide as they come into base. As with any other signal that coaches make, it should be given as early and in as clear a fashion as possible. Though it is helpful to give the advice verbally, it is most important to also give it *visually,* as verbal advice tends to get lost in the uproar of an involved play.

When there is a runner on third base, the coach has the important responsibility of deciding whether or not to send that base runner home on hits to the infield and outfield. Coaches should be very conservative when there are no outs since it is almost impossible not to score a runner from third with no outs. Even with one out, it is better to hold the runner on a hit to the infield or a short fly to the outfield (unless the next batter is a very weak hitter).

Obviously, base coaches need to be alert and calculating. However, there are moments when such an attitude can slip into Machiavillian cunning that may be a shade too much. I once participated in a game in a graduate student league in which one of the teams had a man in a wheelchair who pitched for them. He actually did a very effective job, even managing to field his position reasonably well. However, he was obviously helpless for the most part when a ball was laying on the ground more than a foot or two from him. On one occasion, the play became so heated that he threw himself out of the wheelchair toward a ball that was on the ground, and in doing so he caught his leg in one of the straps of the wheelchair. The coach on the opposing team leaped gleefully in the air and began loudly and aggressively waving his runners around the bases. Some of these runners at least showed a tacit awareness of the inappropriateness of this behavior by running a bit slowly and with their head down while trying to look away from the coach. Nevertheless, they did score the runs (which at this point were unnecessary in winning the game). If anyone ever earned the label "tacky," that coach did.

Le superflu, chose très nécessaire.
The superfluous is very necessary.
Voltaire
(1694-1778)
Le Mondain

Coaching the Drills

There are a number of practices and drills that a coach can direct, or at least initially teach to players. that help improve skills and loosen up a team before a game. Batting effectiveness in a specific game is enhanced by a warm-up period of batting practice wherein each player gets to hit at least five or so balls. This improves timing and removes the anxiety of novelty often experienced by batters coming up to bat for the first time in a game.

The Fungo Drill

After the standard hitting practice the team can then shift into a fungo drill (a practice which is always worthwhile to run through in practice sessions as well as in actual games). In this drill everybody takes the position they typically play (in practice it is worthwhile to occasionally switch people around so that eventually there is always a skilled back-up person for each position—in the event of somebody missing a game, being thrown out of a game, or being hurt).

In a fungo drill, the coach (or pitcher or extra player) who is at home plate, takes the ball from the catcher and in sequence hits ground balls to the third baseman, shortstop, second baseman, and first baseman. In the first round of the drill, each infielder is to throw to first base, except for the first baseman who usually throws to the shortstop covering second, who then may or may not return it to the second baseman covering first. Alternatively, the first baseman may flip it to either the pitcher or second baseman, whomever is covering first, in order to practice those options. In the second phase of the drill, balls are hit again in the same sequence to the various infielders, but they are to convert it into a double play.

In the next part of the drill, fly balls or line drives are hit to the outfielders, and they are to return the ball to second base, third base, and home plate in consecutive parts of the drill. After this, the fungo drill leader may wish to hit balls randomly to the various infielders and outfielders and have them play them as they see fit, responding to cues from their other teammates, just as happens in an actual game.

Other Drills

Of course, there are numerous other drills and practices that a coach can use to develop skills in softball. Many of these can also be practiced by an individual player while alone, though most require the participation of at least a couple of other teammates in order to get the maximum benefit. Just three players can alternate between pitching, batting to a placement area, and having the third person do the fielding. By rotating throughout each position, a person learns each of these skill areas. With a fourth person one can either have an infielder, or use that other person as a catcher/umpire. The catcher/umpire option allows feedback as to whether "balls" or "strikes" are being delivered by the pitcher, and what types of pitches are being hit by the batter. As extra people are added, infielders and/or a first baseman can be placed in sequence.

Base running is seldom practiced, though as noted earlier it is a skill that often needs development. A good practice is to simply run from base to base while attempting to tag the inside of the bases and staying in as a straight a line as possible. It's especially helpful if a stop watch is used for feedback about the time it takes. Similarly, the person can focus on the steps of 1) swinging, 2) dropping the bat, and 3) getting a quick start to first. If another teamates is available, then feedback about technique, in addition to speed, can be obtained. Special attention should be given to getting out of the batter's box quickly. Most players lose more time here than in any other part of the sequence.

People can practice developing speed and accuracy in throws used in the infield just by retrieving balls bounced off of a wall and then throwing to designated spots on the wall. Players can flip the ball off a wall, use this as a mock relay throw from another player, and then turn to throw to a spot on a second wall as a mock target for another baseman.

Outfielders who need to develop throwing skills can simply set up a spot on a wall, or better still, put a keg by a base and attempt to throw into it from various spots in the outfield. This technique can, of course, be modified for infielders such that they throw into a barrel which represents the first baseman. The advantage of these latter exercises is that not only does one get feedback about accuracy, but there is reinforcement, as when the ball goes into the keg one does not have to retrieve it.

Softball is not an exact science.
Prince Bismarck
(1815-1898)
Speech to the Prussian Chamber,
18 Dec. 1963

Coaching and Communication

No matter what approach, philosophy, or practices a coach favors, it's important that as much as possible about these issues be communicated clearly to the team. The greatest disservice is done by a coach who has a clear preference in an area, but who does not communicate it, and then criticizes players who don't perform in accord with that expectancy. Team morale can be very dependent upon the coach's ability to communicate. For example, the philosophy during the season may have been to substitute regularly so that everyone on the team, regardless of ability level, will have gained about equal playing time. But in a championship game, the coach's decision may be to use the best players for this game. This should be communicated ahead of time so that people know what to expect, and are less likely to be upset about it. Ideally, a coach can state a clear description of his or her approach at the beginning of the season, reiterate it on occasion as a reminder, and then most importantly, perform in accord with it.

The best laid schemes o' mice an' men
   fade in the late innings. . .
     Robert Burns
     (1759-1796)
     To a Mouse

Team Evaluation

The initial chapter in this book described several criteria that are useful in selecting and developing a good team. Among these are making sure you have a good shortstop, and picking players who have a good attitude (which depends on what the coaching philosophy is) and who show up dependably for games. It's obviously important to also select on the basis of their skills. One good rule here is "Given two players of about equal skill in softball, choose the better *athlete*." The good athlete has more potential, and will ultimately be more valuable. I hate to say it, but one ought to choose at least some young players, as some team speed is a virtual necessity to a good team, and the young player also has more potential.

A man not old, but mellow, like good wine . . .
     Stephen Phillips
     (1864-1915)
     Ulysses

Hitting and fielding drills and practice games are fine evaluation arenas for assessing specific skills. But the good coach also tries to evaluate a player with any promise in at least one or two actual games. There are a number of "money players" who appear mediocre at best in practice, but then shine in actual games, and especially in clutch situations. Conversely, there are players who look like all-stars in practice, but don't produce in game situations (this latter phenomenon is often the result of anxiety or disruptive thinking, conditions which can usually be helped by some of the techniques described in the upcoming section of this book on Playing the Game Better).

In addition to evaluating individual players, the coach should regularly consider the overall functioning of the team, given the level of competition they are entered in. One worthwhile guideline in such an evaluation is the 7-11 rule.

The 7-11 Rule

The 7-11 rule is a good measure of a team's overall ability. Any team that consistently holds its opponents to *seven or less* runs in a game, and still loses anywhere close to half the games, should reconsider the adequacy of the offense. It's probable that either there is a large "hole" in the batting order, or that players' skills are not being utilized effectively, possibly because of inadequate personnel, the batting order, or other related problems. The remedial strategies noted in the section on "batting" should be reviewed by the coach with that group of team members, and there is probably a need for increased emphasis on batting practice. Team members may need more practice in strategic place-hitting, instead of just hitting anywhere each time. Individual batters should consider whether or not they are hitting too eagerly at the first pitch or trying too often to punch the ball. Also, there should be an examination of whether or not aggressive base running is being used, and of course, some of the weak hitters may need to be replaced with stronger hitters.

On the other hand, any team that scores *eleven* or more runs with consistency, and still loses close to half of the games should look to the adequacy of its defense. Practice, obviously, helps here, but there should also be some reconsideration as to whether players are placed in their optimal defensive positions. On almost any team, a little reshuffling turns out to provide some benefit. Also, the adequacy of the pitching should be re-evaluated. This may be a team where skill in pitching was sacrificed in order to get more offensive punch by using a player who is less skilled as a pitcher yet more potent on offense. As noted earlier, this is a poor strategy, as the pitcher is quite important in slow-pitch softball.

The physical and mental exercises noted in the final and upcoming section of this book may also be used to iron out some of the offensive or defensive problems discussed in this section. They allow individual players, as well as coaches, to perfect (within the limits of athletic ability) the skills detailed in this book.

The conflict between winning and losing is a sickness of the mind.

Seng-Ts'an
Hsin-hsin Ming

3

Playing The Game Better

For our discussion is on no trifling matter, but on the right way to conduct our lives and play softball.
Plato
(429-347 B.C.)
The Republic

In the opening chapter of this book, I described an incident in which a team I played on truly experienced a "Moment of Magic." Everyone was playing without anxiety and at their peak of ability. Such moments occur only when athletes are freed from anxieties about performance (one reason why underdogs often surprise everyone—they have nothing to lose, and thus are not impaired by anxiety). These moments of magic are made possible to the degree one can generate the following conditions:
- the skills are well learned and there is no need for concentration on the minute specifics of a play pattern each time,
- there is comfortable concentration on the overall game itself, without distractions by such things as events external to the game, psych-outs from teammates or opponents, or the athlete's own internal thoughts,
- the athlete is unhampered by anxiety and physiological tension,
- there is a basic experience of enjoyment and satisfaction from that day's participation and performance—even if it does not come close to perfection—there is still a satisfaction with the situation as it is.

The techiques in this chapter are presented as aids to generating these four conditions.

Softball can be played and enjoyed without either long-term or pre-game preparations of any significance. However, just as with most other sports, both the performance level and enjoyment of the game can be enhanced by preparation, and at the same time, the risk of injury can also be lessened through such endeavors. This chapter focuses on various techniques that can help achieve these goals. *However, expert advice (physician, exercise physiologist, physiologist, etc.— depending on the exercise or technique being used) and monitoring on how or what techniques you can use safely should be obtained before engaging in any of the techniques suggested in this section.*

This section is divided into discussion of 1) general preparation methods and 2) pre-game preparation techniques. Within each of these categories, I've detailed at least one primary technique to deal with physical issues while the focus of the other section is on coping with more psychologically-based concerns.

In this first section on general preparation, physical improvement is potentially aided by vision training and by weight training techniques and other exercises that enhance the specific skills commonly used in softball. The psychological technique combines relaxation training and Imagery Rehearsal, methods that have been proven effective in enhancing performance in various sports. This is a research area pioneered by sports psychologists such as Julie Anthony, Ranier Martens, William Morgan, Robert Nideffer, Bruce Ogilvie, and Richard Suinn (Fisher, 1982).

In the section on pre-game preparation, the psychological technique offered is a self-analysis on defusing anxieties and common psych-out techniques. The physical preparation emphasizes a new variant of time-honored stretching exercises, in combination with the standard warm-up procedures of preliminary running, throwing, and batting practice.

General Preparation

It is more blessed to win than to lose.
Acts XX. 35.

Some softballers play the game only very occasionally, and aren't going to care to put in any preparation time to better their performance. Yet, most players will find it worthwhile, in terms of playing better and getting more enjoyment from the game, to try to improve their physical skills and psychological attitudes.

O, it is excellent
To have a giant's strength; but it is tyrannous
To use it like a giant.
William Shakespeare
(1564-1616)
Measure for Measure

Any exercise that improves stamina and/or muscle tone also facilitates performance in virtually any sport, including softball.

Physical Techniques

Before turning to long-term psychological preparation techniques and enhance performance, we'll present some specific physical methods that increase strength and speed in softball. Exercises and techniques which focus on improving flexibility will be discussed in the later section on immediate pre-game physical preparation. Any exercise, (running, calisthenics) that improves stamina and/or muscle tone also facilitates performance in virtually any sport, including softball. However, the following exercises, most of which use weights (or which can be carried out in parallel fashion on a Nautilus machine—see Peterson (1982), are designed to enhance movements prerequisite to the skills required for softball.

Exercise and weight training

In using weight training techniques to increase power and quickness in softball, or in any other sport, there are two essential maxims to always keep in mind:
(1) *Do speed,* and
(2) *Think results.*
This is not to suggest the use of stimulants, as some former drug freaks now turned softballers might assume. Rather, it is to emphasize that one should: a) do the movements in a quick, controlled fashion and b) during performance, also imagine them being carried out in an efficient and explosive (though controlled) manner.

Pain is Gain.
Author prematurely
deceased.

Thus, softballers who aspire to have the power of a Babe Ruth (or Roger Maris) must picture in their mind's eye an overall performance of the movement, their own specific muscle(s) being worked, and the desired results being achieved. This process, once mastered, will transform the drudgery of weight training into a process where power, (strength in combination with speed) greatly enhances athletic performance.

The reason for this is that muscles are made up of both slow twitch (ST) and fast twitch (FT) muscle fibers. Slow twitch (ST) muscle fibers do not tire as easily as do fast twitch (FT) fibers since ST fibers contract more slowly. But on the other hand, while FT fibers tire more quickly, they are critical to any fast muscle movement. A good marathon runner is likely to have less than thirty percent FT muscle fibers and over seventy percent ST muscle fibers. On the other hand, a top sprinter will have less than twenty percent ST fibers and over eighty percent FT fibers. A vertical jump, just jumping straight off the floor without a preparatory step, is a good measure of fast twitch (FT) muscle fiber. Thus, it may not be surprising that top marathon runners often have a vertical jump of less than twenty inches while a good sprinter is usually able to go over twenty-five inches. Surprisingly, most weight lifters have high vertical jumps—the massive Olympic weightlifting champion from the Soviet Union, Alexeev, has a vertical jump of thirty inches (while weighing some 360+ pounds). Herschel Walker, the massive and powerful running back, has a reported vertical jump of forty inches.

FT fibers are those primarily involved in power. Most ball players need power much more than they need simple strength, strength being the ability to move mass without concern for speed of the movement. Power is the addition of speed to strength, and power requires the conditioning of white FT muscle fibers. Slow weightlifting movements, as well as quicker explosive varieties, also use primarily FT fibers.

Unfortunately, the proportion of ST and FT fibers cannot be changed by any nonsurgical techniques, since each one has a different nerve supply. Nevertheless, there is some room for changing the dimensions of the FT fibers themselves through training procedures.

In initiating a weight training program to supplement your softball skills, it is helpful to be familiar with some basic concepts of muscle physiology. The human body is comprised of approximately 600 muscles. Some muscle tissue is exclusively involved in the digestion of our food via the process of peristalsis, while another category of muscle is heart tissue. The third type, skeletal muscle tissue, is used by the body to help the skeletal system affect the environment. In short, the brain sends signals through the central nervous sytem and peripheral nervous system to the muscle via a series of electrical impulses. This process is quite complicated and is effected by a number of factors. It is a command signal which allows the softball player to swing the bat.

Although the skeletal muscles in conjunction with the nervous system control all movement, athletic and otherwise, it should be noted that our muscles are comprised of two different types of muscle fibers, fast twitch (FT) and slow twitch (ST). This distinction is important because the different types of muscle tissue have to be trained in different ways in order to achieve results.

Slow twitch (ST) muscle fibers, or red muscle tissue, are found throughout the body, but the greatest number of fibers are concentrated in those areas in which high repetition work is done, for example, the feet, calves, forearms, and hands. ST fibers contract in such a way so as to not allow for massive and maximum contraction, but the muscles may be worked for extremely long periods of time. Thus an individual can work with his hands or walk great distances without the ST fibers becoming so exhausted that they could no longer squeeze an object or take a step. Yet, ST fibers are limited in that their contractile properties do not readily lend themselves to maximum, one shot exertions. As a result, exercising these body parts must be done in high repetitions of 15-30 per set. Improvement in strength and size can be made in areas primarily comprised of ST fibers, but gains will be smaller, take longer in coming, and can in no way approximate the size and strength gains which can be made in muscles comprised of FT fibers. Doing high repetitions, in fast though controlled movements, and imaging the results in actual softball movements are the keys to success here.

Fast twitch (FT) fiber, or white muscle fiber, is found in comparatively high concentrations throughout the remainder of the body, the thighs, back, chest, shoulders, and upper arms. The physiological properties of FT fibers allow for maximum contraction as found in such activites as sprints, swinging a bat, and throwing a ball. Unfortunately, such muscle tissue becomes exhausted much more readily. Lower repetitions of 3 to 8 per set may be most effectively used in stimulating FT muscle tissue.

Thus, it becomes apparent that there are advantages and disadvantages to each type of tissue. Red muscle tissue (ST) possesses excellent endurance properties, but lacks contractile ability; the opposite is true for white muscle tissue (FT). The number or ratio of FT and ST fibers will vary greatly between individuals. Thus, some people will enjoy great success at endurance activities, while others seem to be more suited to events which are of a short duration and place an emphasis on maximum muscle contraction in their performance. Finally, a number of other factors will influence the relative strength improvement for an individual. Such factors include motivation, health, habits, speed of electrical impulse down the nerve, metabolism, and biomechanical advantage. The latter three factors are directly influenced by the individual's genetic blueprint, as is the ratio of FT and ST fibers.

Greater strength and the potential for increased power occurs as a result of progressive resistance exercise. As a muscle is worked, a very small amount of the muscle tissue is torn down. The body then begins to immediately restore the fatigued tissue. Nutrients are taken from the blood stream and repairs are made. Fortunately for the aspiring softball player, the muscle tissue not only repairs itself, but also slightly adds to the original size of the fatigued muscle. As a result, over time the individual muscle begins to hypertrophy, (grow larger). This process will continue to the person's genetic limits, as long as the resistance (the poundage) used in weight training is increased progressively as strength increases, thus the term progressive weight training.

Most novices at lifting weights are confused about the issue of sets and repetitions. Repetitions are the number of movements done at *one time,* such as 8 repetitions in the press. Sets refer to the number of times an exercise movement is repeated *over time,* such as 5 sets of 5 repetitions in the press. With the goal of softball in mind, it is suggested that the number of sets performed for each exercise range from 3 to 8, while the number of repetitions per set may range from 5 to 10. Thus, a beginner may attempt 3 sets of 10 repetitions, while an advanced weight trainer might do 8 sets of 3 repetitions. Sets and repetitions will vary across individuals and across exercises. Remember to start with a very light weight and progressively add poundage until you are handling a maximum (or near maximum) weight on the last set for that exercise. For example, a beginner might do 3 sets of 8 repetitions on the Bench Press with 50, 75, and 100 pounds, respectively. An experienced weight trainer might handle 120, 140, 160, 180, and 200 pounds on the Bench Press in 5 sets of 5 repetitions. Experimentation, with caution and care so that no injuries occur, best decides the issue.

Those of you who would like greater clarity on how to perform these or similar exercises, or who would like to add exercises, should consult a good book on weight training as it relates to athletics, such as those by Mentzer and Friedberg (1982) or Murrary and Karpovich (1982).

Keeping the prior considerations in mind, the following exercises are suggested, as they are designed specifically for the movements that a softballer would use. *However,* as noted earlier, you should obtain medical clearance before engaging in weight training. I agree with the several experts that assert that teenagers should only work out with weights under close supervision, and that pre-adolescents should not engage in weight training.

For most people, workouts with weights are best done three times a week. This schedule results in consistent development, yet also allows for recuperation of the body on off days (Hooks, 1974). I strongly recommend that you do some stretching exercises (see the later section in this book and either Pat Croce's (1983) book *Stretching for Athletics* or Bob Anderson's (1980) book *Stretching*) before you do any workouts with weights. For Nautilus, see (Peterson, 1983).

The first three exercises suggested provide for overall body development, especially upper body development. We'll then move into exercises that focus on more specific areas related to the strength and power requirements of softball.

1. Bench Press

The Bench Press is perhaps the most important exercise for the upper body. When done properly, it strongly activates the pectorals, triceps, and anterior deltoids. To a lesser extent the posterior and lateral deltoids and latisimus dorsi are also activated. As the largest muscles in the upper body are being worked, noticeable gains in both strength and size should be forthcoming.

Position yourself on the bench with barbell on the uprights. Hand spacing on the bar is optional, but a shoulder width grip might be best for the novice. Experimentation with various width grips will, over time, determine what is best for you. Prior to initiating the lift, grip the bar firmly with both hands; squeeze the bar throughout the exercise. Attempt to keep the wrists as straight as possible. After taking the bar off the rack, pause with the weight at arms length above the chest. Slowly lower the weight until it lightly touches the chest; do not touch the weight after touching the chest, and push the bar to arms length. One round trip constitutes one repetition. Do as many repetitions and sets as your schedule calls for.

Remember to always control the weight and strive for a constant or fluid motion (up and down) throughout the set. Finally, work with maximum weight sets should only be attempted in the presence of a spotter or workout partner. During such maximum sets, it is possible to overestimate your ability and become pinned under the weight. A spotter is necessary in such situations. Should you somehow become pinned without a spotter, do not lie there and hold the weight; you will not find additional strength. Immediately begin to roll the bar down your chest and stomach. Once you reach the thighs then you may sit up and dispose of the weight. If a weight is held too long while contemplating your plight, you may pass out and then the bar may roll onto your neck. Such a situation is frequently terminal when training alone. Individuals who use a bench press machine do not have to worry about this particular risk.

2. Dips

Perhaps one of the best and most underrated exercises for the upper body is the dip. The exercise strongly activates the pectorals, triceps, and anterior deltoid. Less but significant activation also occurs for the lateral and posterior deltoids, trapezius, and latisimus dorsi. With some

A

B

Bench presses develop the muscles of the upper torso.

validity, the dip has been called the "upper-body squat."

Dips are done on any parallel bars. The bars should be 2 to 4 inches wider than shoulder width. As in other exercises the dip is to be performed in a slow controlled fashion while concentrating on the movement, muscles being worked, and results being achieved. After placing oneself upon the dip rack or dip stand, the individual should lower him/herself to a position where the humerus (upper arm) is approximately parallel to the floor. Greater depths should be avoided as it tends to overstretch and aggravate the shoulder joints. *Slightly* hesitate at the bottom of the dip and then push at the bottom of the dip to a fully extended position. Repeat this process for the desired number of repetitions and sets. Remember to keep your back arched throughout the set; this helps to stabilize the body and reduce unwanted sway. To the extent that you lean forward while lowering yourself, a greater emphasis will be placed on the chest muscles. If a more upright position is maintained while lowering yourself, more work is required of the triceps. The choice is yours.

3. Clean and Press

The clean and press is also an excellent exercise for upper body strength. Because a weight is lifted from the floor and extended overhead, numerous major muscle groups are involved. Size and strength gains can be impressive.

This exercise must be divided into two parts: the clean and the press. In cleaning a weight, the goal is to raise a barbell (or set of dumbbells) from the floor to shoulder height. To accomplish this most efficiently, position the shins about 1-2 inches from the bar. Position your hands evenly on the bar at about a shoulder or slightly less than shoulder width. Drop the buttocks, straighten your arms, and arch the back. This is the initial position to start your pull. Ease the bar off the floor using the strength of your thighs and hips. As the bar passes your knees, maintain the arch in your back and begin to accelerate the bar by pulling with the arms. Pull as hard as needed to achieve a maximum height on the bar. At the apex of your pull, rapidly whip your elbows under the bar and rack the bar on your hands and front of the shoulders. Individuals who possess greater shoulder flexibiliy will have greater success in the "racking" portion of the clean movement. After all this work, you are now in a position to initiate your set of presses. At this point you have primarily exercised the muscles of the legs, lower and upper back, and the shoulders to varying extents.

The pressing portion of this movement strongly activates the muscles of the shoulders, triceps, and to a lesser extent, the upper back. To press the weight, position your feet at shoulder width, look straight ahead (not up at the bar) and press the weight overhead. The movement should be controlled and fluid; hesitate at the top or at full extension. Lower the weight to shoulders in the same fashion. This constitutes one repetition. Continue until you have completed the scheduled number of repetitions and sets. At the completion of the set, gently lower the bar to the floor, keeping your back arched, and using the strength of your legs and hips as much as possible.

4. Bent Arm Pullover

In this exercise, lie on a bench with the head supported and with a light barbell held above the chest. Keep the arms straight up in the air at a right angle to the body. Gradually bend the arms as the weight of the barbell is lowered to a position behind the head and down below a plane that is level with the bench. Then raise the bar back to the starting position. The bar should be grasped with the palm up and with the fingers pointed behind the head. Start out with three sets of six repetitions if this feels reasonably comfortable. Based on general feelings of body comfort, gradually work up to eight sets of five repetitions, emphasizing speed and consistent good form. This exercise works the muscles used in throwing as well as some of the muscles used in hitting. A variation of this exercise can be carried out on a wall pulley. This exercise apparatus has ropes and pulleys to pull up the weights as the person exercising pulls out on the rope and handle. A throwing motion (though not a hard or fast one) can be mimicked on this machine.

5. Weighted Shrugs

To develop power in throwing, a good exercise is a forward and upward shrugging of the shoulder while holding a moderate weight barbell and pushing out to a straight arm position from an original position where the barbell is held over the chest and close in by the shoulder. In an alternative exercise, the hands (holding the weight) remain close in to the shoulders. The shoulders are alternately brought forward, and then up, and then subsequently lowered, and back up and around. Try to cover as wide a range of shoulder movement as possible, again without moving the rest of the body, and without jerky movements.

6. Pull Downs

This exercise is easily carried out on the slightly curved bar found on most Universal weight training machines. Using a moderate amount of weight, the bar is grasped at the ends so that the arms form a wide V above the head. The bar is then pulled down *behind the head* to a position resting on the neck, and the bar is then returned to the original position. If this machine is not available, a stationary chin-up bar can be used by performing behind-the-head pull-ups on this bar. Try to achieve three sets of eight repetitions at the start, and eventually and comfortably work up to eight sets of five repetitions each. This exercise works on muscles used in both throwing and hitting.

An alternative form of this exercise involves pulling the bar down *in front of the face to the neck.* While the behind-the-head form works more on the chest muscles, this alternative form works more on the rear shoulder and back muscles.

7. Crossovers

Again using a wall pulley, stand with your right arm and side toward the wall, and with your left arm and side away from the wall. Reach across with your left hand, grasp the pulley, and pull. Start your left hand at the lower chest area and pull up and across to a straight out position with your left arm now extended straight away from the wall. This exercises those muscles in the left arm that are specific to the standard motion when swinging a bat. It is, however, worthwhile to do this exercise both with the left and right arms so as not to facilitate asymmetric muscle development. Try to do this for five repetitions with each arm in each of three sets, and gradually build up to ten sets of five repetitions.

If a wall pulley is not available, this exercise may be carried out by laying on a bench on your right side and then grasping a dumbbell with the left hand; lowering it across the body and down below the bench and then swinging the weight straight up so that it is extended directly above the body. Switch positions to work both arms, and again do the number of repetitions suggested above. This movement mimics the forward arm of a person swinging a bat. Remember that it is helpful not only to do this with *moderate* speed in the actual movement, but also envision swinging the bat with speed as you make the movement.

8. Flies

In this exercise, you lie on a bench with a dumbbell in each hand. Lower the dumbbells to just slightly below a horizontal plane with the rest of the body and directly out at a 90 degree angle from the body on each side, but do keep the arms slightly bent throughout. Then raise them, but not too quickly, up to a direct overhead position so that you are looking straight up through a small space between the two dumbbells, and then lower them again. Do a first set of eight repetitions and work up to four sets. This helps develop the strength required in the back of the arms in order to swing a bat with the power. It also facilitates throwing and to a lesser degree the forward arm movements used in swinging a bat.

9. Wrist curls

These are best carried out by sitting on a bench or chair. While grasping a dumbbell, put the elbow on the thigh, and allow the forearm to drop over the knee with the wrists held slightly below the knee. The dumbbell is raised from this position below the knee up to as high a position as is comfortable, *using only the wrist to make the movement and curling the dumbbell in toward the bicep.* The dumbbell is then lowered and raised for 12-15 repetitions, gradually building up to ten sets.

I have also found the "Nautilus" wrist exercise unit put out by Sports/Medical Industries to be an inexpensive and useful aid to the development of wrist strength, though the action here is more of a twist than a curl. Again, and with either technique, envision a movement in which the wrist whips the bat into a powerful swing.

10. Wrist Pronater

Another technique that specifically develops the wrists as well as some of the forearm and hand muscles is the "wrist pronater." A dumbbell with the weights left on only one one end is used in this technique. The forearm is rested on a table and the dumbbell is held in the same way that a bat would be, with the weight on the dumbbell held in the direction where the end of the bat would be. The hand is moved back and forth from a palm up position (though the fist is curled over the handle of the dumbbell handle) and then flopped over to where the palm would be facing down if the fists were extended (referred to as a pronated position). Do one complete flip-flop for approximately 15 repetitions in three sets with each hand, and build up from there to about 30 repetitions in five sets. However, as with all of these exercises, keep away from any excessive strain.

11. Squeezers

Not only is wrist strength very important, but grip strength is likewise essential to delivering power to the bat. If the person has a weak grip, much of the strength built up in any other area is lost in the swing. The grip can be built up by squeezing rubber balls of various sizes that have a moderate degree of give. Using balls of different sizes allows hand strength to be increased throughout a greater range of movements. At the very minimum do this for several minutes with each hand. Many people find it helpful to carry a few rubber balls with them in the car and then to do this exercise when they are stuck in traffic. *Don't do the exercise while actually driving.* There are a variety of other devices that are marketed for this purpose, and they do help to develop hand strength, but there is no evidence that they are more effective than using rubber balls.

Another method of increasing grip strength gained attention through its practice by a local arm-wrestling champion in Southern California. He would, with *one* hand, pick up a Galliano Italian liqueur bottle, a very long slender shape, filled with pennies, and with the bottle held horizontally, work it through his hand from end to end without his hand or the bottle touching anything. If you can do that, you have no problem with grip strength. To show off he would then crush three bottle caps between the first knuckles of his four fingers. One friend tried to trick him by gluing a dime under the cork of one of the bottle caps. Our arm-wrestler blinked momentarily at the extra resistance, and then crushed that cap as well.

Tender handed stroke a softball
And it stings you for your pains
Grasp the bat like a man of mettle.
>   Aaron Hill
>   (1685-1750)
>   *Verses written on a*
>   *window in Scotland*

During a light moment in the dugout, Cobbie Harrison, of the Jiffy Cafe (and later of the Kentucky Bourbons Pro Slo-Pitch team), demonstrates a free-form arm-wrestling technique to build up wrist strength.
Photo courtesy of ASA

12. Squats

In softball, as well as with many other athletic endeavors, the primary source of power comes from the hips, legs, and lower back. This is especially so in hitting. A crucial source of power in hitting derives from the rotary motion of the hips, which deliver the power from the mass of the body into the swing and then into the bat. Squats are a major way of developing both this mass and power. Place the barbell on the shoulders behind the head and keep the back as upright as possible and the heels on the floor. Then lower into a squat position going down only so far that the top of the thighs are parallel with the floor (do not go lower than this); then rise up. Do not bounce out of the bottom of this position; it can result in injury. Rather, go fluidly back up into the rise.

There are two variations of the squat, and they seem to develop slightly different muscle groups. In the first variation, the butt and hips protrude out toward the back as the exercise is carried out, resulting in more development of the muscles in the upper thighs, and especially in the back of the legs and in the hips. In the second variation, the hips and butt are kept flat with the back, resulting in more development of the front thigh muscles. This second varition is more similar to the development one gains from a leg press on a Universal machine. Start with five repetitions in three sets with the butt and hips protruding out back, and the same with the butt and hips as flat as possible with the back. Gradually work up to eight repetitions and 5-8 sets of each.

It is best to vary the weight in the squats throughout the three exercise days in the week. Use a very light weight one day, a medium weight the next, and a heavy weight on the third. Then, on the following week again return to a light, medium, heavy sequence, based on the amount of weight that is both comfortable and moderately demanding at that time. You may wish to vary the repetitions and sets each of these days, based on the weight and your personal comfort.

13. *Rotary Action Development*

As noted, it is important to develop strength in the rotary movements that deliver power from the legs and hips up into the arms and then into the bat. One friend of mine has reported substantially increased strength in this rotary action by making the batting movement in a swimming pool with the water up to the neck. He goes through the actual batting motion, *but in both directions to maintain symmetry of development.* He does this for approximately thirty repetitions each way, emphasizing both the rotary movement and thinking speed and results.

There are also some additional weight training methods to help in this rotary power development. In the *Back Oblique Raise,* the lifter lies face down on a bench and slightly on his side so that the body is at a 45 degree angle with the bench. The feet are well supported and the rear end is near the end of the bench. The body is allowed to go all the way down flat on the bench and then is raised up until it is almost at a 90 degree angle with the bench. It is important to do this exercise (8 repetitions, up to 4 sets each way) from both sides to maintain symmetry of power development. The hands are held across the chest and if more weight is desirable to aid in development here, a dumbbell can be held at the chest in this exercise. After this, you can move into the *Front Oblique Raise* which is done in exactly the same manner as the *Back*

Oblique Raise, only the lifter now lies *face up* and exerts the same movements.

Another specific exercise for increasing strength in this torsion movement is the *Hip Swing.* Take a barbell of low to moderate weight for you and hold it behind the back approximately 1/3 to 1/2 up the back, lodged in the crook of each elbow. The hands of each arm are brought around toward the front of the body in order to hold the barbell firm. While in this position, swing as you would when batting. Alternate swinging in *both* directions to develop the oppositional sets of muscles; start at three minutes, and work up to ten minutes.

Ken Curtis demonstrates ideal batting form as he shifts his power off of the back foot and through the hips while keeping his eye on the ball. When not doing this sort of thing, he served as the Governor of Maine.
Photo courtesy of <u>Balls</u>
<u>and Strikes</u> and the ASA

14. Toe Presses

Given the movement requirements in softball, it is worthwhile also to add power to the calf muscles as this complements the power from the thighs. Using the same barbell position as in the squat, the bar being held behind the head and resting on the neck, raise quickly up to full height on the toes and then go down, but not too quickly. You should not feel the weight bouncing down as you go back to a flat footed position. Do this for 15 to 20 repetitions, gradually building up to four sets. The calf muscles can also be worked by pressing on the plate on a Universal machine,

144

which allows variations in the effort being expended.

There are several other techniques that develop power, and they even more closely approximate the actual movements used in throwing and hitting.

Every Communist must grasp the truth.
'Political power grows out of the
barrel of a bat.'
Mao Tse-Tung
(1893-1976)
Selected Works

15. Weighted Bat

Swinging a weighted bat is an excellent way of developing power in the swing. At the same time, this can be combined with hitting a ball off a batting tee in order to develop timing as well as power. The most economical and efficient way to do this is to take a discarded bat (either because it is broken or because it just doesn't work at all for you) and then drill a hole in it into which hot lead is poured. Old fishing weights can be melted for this purpose, or lead can be obtained cheaply from most hardware stores. It does not require particularly high heat (but some caution) to melt the lead. Bats with different weights can be made up so that one can move up to a very heavy bat in approximate steps during each session or season. The weighted bat is helpful not only for use in regular workouts, but for warming up before a game and before times at bat as well. It does wonders for your hitting if you forget and proceed to bat with it (but only if you are not discovered by the umpire).

16. Weighted Ball

Just as a weighted bat is helpful in developing power in the batting motion, a weighted ball is effective in developing throwing strength. An old ball is drilled and again filled with hot lead. Also, as in the prior technique, you can do this with a number of balls, varying the weight up to 10 or 12 ounces of lead.

If making up balls this way strikes you as weird or tedious, you could use shotputs of various sizes, possibly starting with a five pound model, and gradually move up. *Be aware that this exercise can be rough on the elbow and shoulder joints,* and if you have (or had) problems in these areas (such as trauma or inflammation) only engage in this exercise after medical clearance.

17. Wrist Snap

Many batters never develop a quick and effective wrist snap in their swing. This is unfortunate since it is the wrist snap that delivers a tremendous amount of power to the ball. The greater the strength and the control in the wrist snap, the more potent the batter. One technique to develop this is to take a bat and drill a hole in the end of it, approximately 1 to 2 inches from the end of the bat. Then drill a hole through the center of a ball and connect the two with some heavy nylon string or with wire, keeping the ball approximately 5 to 6 inches from the bat. Then swing the bat with the hole from which the string is extended to the ball being to your rear or back. As you swing, the ball will flip in front of the bat at the point the wrist is snapped. This gives direct feedback on the snap; where it occurs, how fast it is made, and at the same time this motion can help to increase power. Some people report good results from combining this with the weighted bat technique.

To reiterate, only do these exercises *after medical clearance*. Also, if you experience any pain or distress, stop and consult a physician before proceeding.

As noted elsewhere in this book, feedback is an effective way to learn in any endeavor. So it is occasionally useful in any exercise to have someone comment on your swing or movement, and in that way help you to improve it. Some obtain this feedback by practicing the swing in front of a mirror, though this can be slightly distracting in a swing since you will be watching the mirror instead of peering out to a distance where the pitcher theoretically would be. For those who wish a bit more sophistication, video tapes of the hitting style and stance can be made. These offer precise feedback, as well as a record for comparison with a later swing. This earlier record becomes especially valuable when there is an apparent loss of rhythm in the swing. The tapes are helpful for modeling a return to the more effective swing.

The doctor confirmed the hernia and shouted to my mother in the next room, "My God, he's shaved his pubes!" . . . I promised God that I'd do just about anything for Him if He'd fix the problem. That week I hit a grand-slam homerun during lunch-hour recess and ripped my gut so badly I couldn't walk for three days. (p. 71)
Bill Henderson
My Son (1982)

Vision Training

As noted elsewhere, in this book, Ted Williams' skill (not to mention his power) in batting is legendary. His consistently high average, even including one amazing season when he hit .406, certainly validates the legend. Many felt that abnormally acute vision was the reason for such performance since allegedly he could discriminate the stitches on a blazing fastball as he struck it with his bat, and he could read the words

146

on signs when others couldn't even find the sign.

Such stores do help legends to develop, but Williams debunked these beliefs. Williams once wrote "Hitting a baseball—I've said it a thousand times—is the single most difficult thing to do in sport.... I sure couldn't read labels on revolving phonographs as people wrote I did. I couldn't 'see' the bat hit the ball, another thing they wrote, but I knew the feel of it. A good carpenter doesn't have to see the head of the hammer strike the nail but he still hits it square every time." (Pesmen, p. 19).

Yet, overall visual skills are critical to good hitting skills in baseball or softball, and for most sports. The great majority of relevant information that people take in during life comes in through the eye. The useful information taken in through the eye by a player during a softball game is even higher, maybe as much as 90%, and in hitting it approaches 100%. The process itself is rather simple, at least from an overview perspective (Marr, 1982). Information, in the form of various light wave patterns passing through the cornea, is filtered by the iris (which controls the size of the opening for the light, the pupil). The filtered information passes through the vitreous humor (a gooey fluid), having been focused by the lens of the eye to strike the retina, and the information patterns registered by the retina are passed by the optic nerve to the brain. There they are integrated with relevant information from other sensory inputs and memory. The eyeballs are controlled by six muscles: the superior and inferior rectus muscles allow the eyeball to move up and down, the lateral and medial rectus muscles move the eyeball from side-to-side, and the superior and inferior oblique muscles control torsion movements (Kavner & Dusky, 1978).

Williams attributed his success in batting to discipline in following the ball (in addition to a classic swing). In actuality, the visually based skills of batting can be broken down into four components, which are 1) sound eyesight, 2) a trained ability to keep the eyes on the ball through the entire target sequence, a skill referred to as binocularity, 3) maximal eye muscle training to optimize the amount of information taken in by the eye, and 4) appropriate eye dominance. While there are built in limits as to how much one can improve these components, definite improvement can be attained in all four areas (Marr, 1982; Kavner & Dusky, 1978).

1. Sound vision—Simple as it may seem, the very first thing to do is learn the capabilities and limits of one's own eyesight. Curtis Pesmen (1983) relates the story of how Arthur Ashe, the world renowned tennis player discovered his limits. In 1964, Ashe found himself squinting to see road signs as he drove down the Baja highway in California toward Tijuana. The kicker was that he realized that his fellow tennis pro, Charlie Pasarell, was reading them easily. Ashe consulted an eye doctor, and had his vision corrected, at which point his career took off. He won the

U.S. Open at Forest Hills and was named number one tennis player in the world four years later.

So the first rule is to make sure your eyes are functioning at maximum efficiency. As I can personally testify, this becomes even more critical as one passes age thirty-five. Some male players feel it looks too sissy-like to wear glasses when playing. Of course, contacts can solve that hang-up for many, but if contacts are not feasible for some reason, remember the adage that sissies who can see do hit (and play) better than macho squinters.

Various exercises can also be used to improve the condition of the eyes, especially the tone of the eye muscles. A simple but effective exercise is to regularly alternate focusing the eyes for several seconds on objects in the corners, center, and other random points in the visual field. Also, vary this exercise by occasionally alternating between near and far objects. As with this or any other exercises, if there is excessive discomfort or unusual side-effects, immediately stop the exercise, and consult a specialist. Frankly, it is wise (no matter what your age) to have a good eye examination, at the very least just to know your strengths and weaknesses, before trying for improvement with any of these exercises.

2. _Following the ball_—Efficiency of vision as well as binocularity (the coordination of both eyes to bring moving objects into focus) can also be improved. First, obtain a pair of Polaroid glasses, and if necessary, tape or tie them to your head so that they stay fast. Now, jump up and down (and turn around in random patterns) while throwing a ball at a target on a wall from the assorted positions that result. Remember to keep your eyes focused on the target whenever at all possible. Some prefer to vary this exercise by just bouncing up and down on a mini-trampoline while throwing the ball, but some of the Loonies tend to fall off the trampoline, so exercise considerable caution here. This type of exercise coordinates eye focusing with body movement, a critical skill in virtually all sports (Kavner & Dusky, 1978).

3. _Concentration and coordination_—The above exercises should improve general concentration and coordination, but there are several other exercises that also specifically promote eye-hand coordination. Throwing a ball high up in the air in dim light and catching it in various positions is a good one, but use a tennis ball so you don't give yourself a lobotomy when you miss an especially high throw. Another and more difficult exercise involves attempting to repetitively bat a ball (again, a tennis ball) against a wall, just as one might do in practicing tennis against a wall. You can make it even tougher by doing it in a darkened room with only a strobe light on. No strobe light!—well, just blink your eyes rapidly, this generates the same effects.

4. Eye dominance—While we see with both eyes, our dominant eye is the one we *aim* with. Donald Teig did research (Pesman, 1983) to support the idea that batters are slightly more efficient if their dominant eye is the one closest to the pitcher.

How can you tell which eye is dominant? Teig suggests this easy test. Pick a spot about twenty feet away. Now, with both eyes open and arms outstretched and palms down, bring your hands together at eye level so that they overlap and still leave a small triangle that frames the spot you picked out. Freeze that position for a moment and then close one eye. If that specific spot is blocked out, this is your nondominant eye, if it's still there, it's your dominant eye.

Unfortunately, most of us are right-eye dominant and bat right-handed. It is almost impossible, and certainly not advisable, to try to change your eye dominance. Also, the gain in efficiency (against the loss in strength and experience) would not warrant changing batting position for most players. However, for right-eye dominant youngsters, it would be just one more reason to start off batting left-handed.

We've now considered a number of physical methods that are useful in long-term preparation to play the game better. Let's turn to some psychological techniques that have the same goal.

Believe me! The secret of reaping the greatest fruitfulness and the greatest enjoyment from life is to play softball and live dangerously.
Friedrich Nietzsche
(1844-1900)
Die Fröhliche Wissenschaft

Psychological Techniques

A variety of psychological factors impinge on performance in any sport. In this regard, for those of you who are seriously into softball or some other sport, it may be worthwhile to take the Sports Emotional Reaction Profile, a 42 item questionnaire designed by one of the pioneers in sport psychology in America, Thomas Tutko, and which is reprinted in his 1976 book. Like many questionnaires, the items are rather apparent in what they are trying to assess. So it is important to take it in as open and honest a fashion as possible, responding neither in the direction of downplaying issues nor exaggerating them. This questionnaire gives a score on seven separate psychological areas that bear on athletic performance: Desire, Assertiveness, Sensitivity, Tension Control, Confidence, Personal Accountability, and Self Discipline. Tutko goes on to describe issues that might be worthwhile to consider in relation to high or low scores on these specific characteristics. The test is included in his book, so it is easy to take it, and then reflect on it in terms of what you may want to achieve in athletics.

In this section of the present book, some psychological techniques for improving performance are presented. Imagery Rehearsal (IR) helps perfect the various behavioral skill patterns that lead to better play. Autogenic Training (AT), a form of relaxation training, has been shown to facilitate the practice of Imagery Rehearsal, and in addition, helps lessen the build-up of tension and apprehension that can interfere with performance in sports. The techniques of Defusing Thoughts helps get rid of specific negative ongoing thoughts, such as "I just know I'll never be any good at this," that often disrupt effectiveness, especially in clutch situations.

We have first rained a dust and then complain we cannot see.
Bishop Berkeley
(1685-1753)
Principles of Human Knowledge

Imagery Rehearsal (IR)

Imagery rehearsal (IR) is a technique in which a person rehearses various skills through images that they generate and maintain in their own mind. IR has been used to perfect athletic skills, as well as to develop more general skills that make for effective and happier living. The use of this technique for athletes was pioneered primarily by several sports psychologists, including Richard Suinn (1980), and he uses a term that he originated, called "Visuo-Motor Behavior Rehearsal" (VMBR). He as well as a number of others have reported success with the general technique throughout a wide range of different athletic skills (Nideffer, 1981; Cratty, 1983). I use the more generally applicable term Imagery Rehearsal (IR), because the rehearsal is actually done with images rather than with any specific behaviors.

The potency of this technique is even greater if senses other than vision are brought into the development of the images. For example, one might clearly imagine the full sequence of throwing a new type of pitch, such as a knuckleball, with precise control and positive effects in imagined game situations. This is the essence of IR. If, however, the image is enhanced by calling up in one's mind the common sounds of the softball game or sensations of warmth from the sun or even smells often associated with the game, the imagery is enhanced and the effect produced is greater.

Some of the effects from Imagery Rehearsal have been truly astounding. Robert Titley (Suinn, 1980) reports one example in an article termed the "The Lonelines of a Long-Distance Kicker." It all started in the fall of 1973 when the Colorado State football team found itself without an adequate placekicker. The coach advertised in the student newspaper, and one of the people who turned out showed some promise, a fellow who had never played much football though he had played a lot of soccer. By the seventh game of that season, after some thorough and careful instruction, this kicker, Clark Kemble, began to show progress and produced some adequate performances. Then in the third game of the next season, he missed a field goal in the closing minutes of a tight battle with Memphis State, and Colorado State lost 20-18. Then he missed a long conversion (as a result of a penalty) in the next game, a point that then would have broken a tie and won the game for Colorado State. Though he kicked three field goals early in the next week's game, he missed a fourth try from 29 yards out and Colorado State lost that one 24-23.

It was at this time that the coach, fairly sophisticated about the possibilities of sports psychology, brought in Doctors Suinn and Titley to work on the problem.

The kicker underwent the Imagery Rehearsal, and was apparently a very good subject. Clark was able to relax fully and develop vivid imagery, both important predictors of high success with this technique. In the game following the primary treatment sessions, he kicked nine out of nine extra points and one out of one field goals. The sessions, originally held almost daily, were now continued on a once-a-week basis. The following week he kicked three field goals, all over 40 yards in distance on a slippery field, and they provided the margin of victory in an 11-6 game with Wyoming. He continued to kick well the rest of that season.

When Clark returned in the following season, still continuing with the IR, he consistently kicked long and accurately and provided the margin of victory in several games. During that season, Colorado State played Air Force Academy, whose kicker then held the NCAA major college distance record for field goal kicking at 62 yards. Clark, in anticipation of the match-up, practiced hard with the IR in the week before the game. On that Saturday, he put nine kickoffs into or beyond the end zone, kicked four field goals of 26, 29, 40, and 53 yards, and made five of five extra points. He had outdueled Air Force's vaunted kicker. Unfortunately, Clark's fifth field goal fell five yards short—it was attempted from 67 yards outs.

In the next game against Arizona, Clark gave Colorado State (a decided underdog) a 3-0 lead with a 47 yard kick early in the game. Then, in the second quarter, Colorado State was trailing 7-3, and had driven to the Arizona 46 yard line, but stalled there. Clark went out to attempt a field goal under intense pressure in front of a deathly silent crowd. The kick was long, accurate, and beautiful to watch—63 yards away and over the goal posts, a new NCAA major college record.

Elements in IR

The key factors in Imagery Rehearsal are the development of both vivid images and a preliminary state of relaxation. These images ideally include all the senses that are feasible, such as smell, hearing, muscular sensations, and even the probable accompanying emotional reactions. It is more than simple imagination. Rather, when it is most effective, it is a true copy of experience, a sort of body thinking experience that reminds those who practice it of the powerful illusion induced by certain dreams and nightmares. Of course, in Imagery Rehearsal (IR), the subject of the images is under conscious control.

There is some controversy as to whether or not a state of relaxation is really needed to effectively carry out Imagery Rehearsal. However, most do agree that the subjects are less inclined to be distracted if they are relaxed, and therefore are more easily able to develop powerful and vivid images. For that reason, I always recommend inclusion of a preliminary stage of relaxation training before going into IR itself. At the end of this section I will present an outline of a technique called Autogenic Training, which I have modified for use with Imagery Rehearsal.

There are two factors within the IR practice itself that contribute substantially to long term success: (1) the development of *vivid* images, (2) using only the imagination of *optimal or ideal* behaviors in the Imagery Rehearsal.

As already noted, developing vivid images is helped by relaxation training, and also to the degree the person can bring in images from more than one sense. Developing vivid images sometimes can be facilitated by allowing actual physical movements to happen, rather than trying to sit still or lay down in a prone position without moving. One player who I worked with developed more vivid images to the extent that he was allowed to move into a batting stance and start to take an imaginery grip on a bat. He didn't actually feel it necessary to make a swing with the imagined bat, and once when he tried that he found it to be distracting. But at least a partial degree of actual muscle involvement enhanced his success.

In the early years of the development of IR, there was not much emphasis on generating optimal behavior images. However, it is now quite clear that this is critical to succeess. Whenever you proceed through any imagined behavior sequence in Imagery Rehearsal, always see yourself doing it *as you would ideally like to do it,* not as you usually do it.

To practice IR effectively, the first move is to pick out the skill to be improved on, such as batting. The next step is to break down this action into smaller sequences of behavior, for instance, deciding if one is going to wait for a certain pitch versus planning to hit a good pitch in a direction dictated by the pitch itself. Separately and graphically envision each step: taking a stance, getting the bat into proper position, preparing to effectively move forward off the back foot to deliver power into the hips and then into the arms, all the while watching the pitcher deliver the ball, experiencing fully the swing itself, seeing the ball clearly as it approaches and then is struck with the bat, and lastly, perceive and feel a complete follow through.

The next step is to think carefully through an ideal sequence incorporating these separately imagined elements. The majority of athletes find this the most effective way to do Imagery Rehearsal (IR). Begin with parts of the sequence imagined individually, and later combine all of them into one full image sequence. Certainly, at some point in each session, the full sequence of behaviors should be practiced, as it is then easier to bring in all of the senses to enhance the image process.

After Autogenic Training (described in the next section) has brought on an acceptable level of relaxation, I suggest the practice of Imagery Rehearsal (IR) of each skill to be improved for approximately five minutes each day for the first week for each skill. Then, gradually, by one extra minute per day increase it to ten minutes for each skill. After two weeks of practicing it approximately five to seven times per week (we all procrastinate somewhat), I recommend cutting back to only two or three times per week.

A danger to avoid while practicing IR is becoming obsessed with trying to do it "perfectly," (though the images themselves should be of a relatively ideal pattern). Many people become too caught up in whether or not they have practiced it for the exact aount of time, whether their images were vivid enough, or whether they allowed too many distractions. The fact is that all of us have good sessions and bad sessions—the idea is: 1) simply to try to do one's best, 2) keep a reasonable check on whether the behavior envisioned is an optimal one (possibly by discussions with a tutor in this method), and 3) practice with persistence but not with an obsessive or overly critical attitude. *As with any other practice or technique in this book, if distress or any other disturbing side-effect develops, stop the practice, and consult an expert in that area.*

In addition to the IR, one should, of course, also engage in real world practice of the behaviors. This allows your cognitive practice in the IR to flow into actual behavior and become a well-learned physical pattern. In this vein, remember that one of the best ways to avoid anxiety about performance is an old tried and true method—simply learning through practice (and now Imagery Rehearsal) the pattern so well that it becomes automatic and fluid. An overlearned behavior can usually override the disruptive potential of mild and even moderate negative thoughts or anxiety.

'Tis a lesson you should heed,
Try, try again.
If at first you don't succeed,
Try, try again.
    W.E. Hickson
    (1803-1870)
    Try and Try Again

Autogenic Training (AT)

Autogenic training (AT) is a relaxation training method based on a significant body of research. The basic ideas in Autogenic Training were developed in the early 1900's in Germany by Oscar Vogt and then Wolfgang Luthe, and were subsequently thoroughly researched, particular in Europe, and have now spread throughout the world. The research indicates AT can lower anxiety, tension, and stress. This has numerous positive benefits physiologically (Meyer 1983), and specific to our purposes here, it directly facilitates the practice of Imagery Rehearsal.

The following sections on the positions, training elements, and the exercises themselves should provide a thorough overview of how to practice the Autogenic Training method of relaxation development. There are a variety of other ways to develop a relaxation response (E. Jacobson's (1964) "Progressive Relaxation" technique). Any of these would suffice to facilitate Imagery Rehearsal. However, since I personally feel that Autogenic Training (AT) is at least as effective, if not more so, than other techniques, I'll present it in detail here.

Positions in AT

The Prone Position: The great majority of people find that the most efficient way to learn and experience results from AT is to do the exercises while lying down. The following suggestions help most people maximize their results. But these comments are not to be read as hard and fast rules, and can be modified to individual needs. Do these exercises only insofar as they are benefiting you. Do not persist, without the advice of an expert, if you experience pain or other forms of distress.

While lying down, the legs are usually slightly apart and relaxed so that the feet are inclined outward at a V-shaped angle. The trunk, shoulders, and head are most easily relaxed when kept in a symmetric position. The arms should lie relaxed and slightly bent beside the trunk of the body. The fingers remain slightly spread and flexed and generally do not touch the rest of the body.

Attention should be given to determining the most relaxing position for the head, neck and shoulders. It's advised that different pillows be tried to see which is most comfortable for these exercises. If there is a continuing stiffness in the neck or shoulder muscles during the exercises, consider whether or not the pillow is both soft and yet supportive enough. While doing the exercises in the prone position, it is advisable that shoes be removed. When a blanket is used, it should not be tightly wrapped around any part of the body since pressure may have a distracting effect during the exercise. Another point, and one that's frequently overlooked, is that certain people relax more completely and perform the exercises more effectively when given some support (a folded blanket) under the knees.

The Reclining Chair Position: The autogenic exercises can also be performed in any type of reclining chair that has a high enough back so that the trunk and head can rest comfortably. Most of the comments made for the prone position are also relevant here. However, in a surprising number of instances reclining chairs provide postures that are not as comfortable as may first appear. You should feel free to use pillows and other means of adjusting the contours of the chair so that it provides a comfortable position. It is best if there is support throughout the length of both the arms and the legs.

The Straight Chair Position: In this position, seldom used unless a bed or recliner is not available, the edge of the seat should not exert pressure on the legs, and the feet should rest solidly on the ground. In order to attain a position of maximal relaxation in this position, you should first of all straighten up completely while you are in the sitting position. Then with both arms hanging down at the sides, suddenly relax completely, which results in a kind of collapse of the trunk, shoulders, and neck. Thus, the body is now supported primarily by the skeleton and ligament structure. It's best to keep the back relatively straight; in other words, the trunk collapses downward without bending forward. To the degree possible, the body should feel as if it's hanging loose. Most find it ideal to have the underside of the forearms rest on the upper thighs. The head drops forward and the arms, although touching the legs, feel as if in a loose position.

Training Elements in AT

Passive Concentration: Autogenic Training proceeds most efficiently for people when they approach it with an attitude best described as "passive concentration." Passive concentration may be explained by contrasting it to active concentration. The decisive difference between active concentration and passive concentration is the attitude toward the functional results to be achieved. Active concentration is characterized by a concern and even active efforts to try to make the result come about during that particular exercise. This should be avoided as this often generates anxiety about performing well. Passive concentration, on the other hand, implies a casual attitude and a passivity toward the intended outcome of the autogenic exercises on that particular day. This, of course, doesn't mean that you don't hope for positive results as an eventual outcome of the exercises. But, during that particular exercise, you should try to eliminate a need to see any dramatic results.

Steady Flow of Images: A second important element in autogenic training is maintaining a steady flow of mental images that represent the autogenic formulae (provided later in this section). Do not allow lapses of time to occur between your repetitions of the formulae. Rather, keep repeating them in a slow but continuous fashion. This steady flow of images may be provided by your "inner voice," or by visualizing the particular formulas as if they are in print, or as if they are a neon sign in the mind which can be switched on and off at will. It is not particularly critical which method is used to maintain this steady flow of images. However, it is important that once you have decided on which form (inner voice, visual image, etc.) is most comfortable for you that you stay with it throughout the training. Also, you should not speak the words aloud.

Mental Contact: Mental contact refers to putting the attention of your mind in touch with the particular body part that is the focus of whichever formula you are then imagining. If you are using the formula "my right arm is heavy," it is important to try to imagine you are mentally in touch with your arm. Some people even image themselves as being their arm. Whichever way works best with you is fine. However, from long-term experience, it's clear that the functional value of the formulae is markedly enhanced to the degree there is not only a steady flow of images, but also consistent mental contact with the part of the body that is the area of focus. The flow of images should, of course, be kept in pace with the formula being repeated.

Reduction of Stimuli: Autogenic training is always most successful when external stimuli are reduced to the lowest possible level during the procedures. To the degree available, the exercises should be practiced in a quiet room with low lighting, if any. No matter what position the person takes, all restrictive clothing (glasses, belt, girdle, necktie, etc.) should be either loosened to a point of comfort or else removed.

A further reduction of external stimuli is gained by *closing the eyes.* It is desirable to do this as soon as the posture is taken, no matter which posture is used. From a number of studies, it is well known that there is a positive correlation between the phenomenon of eye-closure and the attainment of relaxation.

Preparing for the possibility of other types of external distractions is also helpful in facilitating AT. You might consider taking the phone off the hook to avoid having a phone call occur during the AT exercises. Also, it's best not to do AT when you are under some time pressure. Don't lay down to do them when you know you only have a few minutes before you could be interrupted by an appointment or visit. The anticipation of possible interruption usually causes a distraction from the passive concentration and mental contact requirements.

Time in Practice: A practice period is generally made up of 5 to 8 subunits of practice. During the initial phases of AT, it is preferable to restrict each subunit of the exercises to approximately one minute. That is, all of the formulae that you have been working on up to this point are practiced for approximately 60 seconds (there is no need to be obsessive about making it exactly 60 seconds). After each subunit of the exercises, you should bring yourself back to a normal feeling state by:
● Opening your eyes
● Flexing your arms and legs rather vigorously
● Breathing deeply.
After carrying this out, return to the position you have chosen and carry out another subunit of the exercises for approximately 60 seconds. Keep repeating this until you have performed 5 to 8 subunits, and then proceed into Imagery Rehearsal.

The AT Exercises

The Overall Formula: while most of the formulae that you will gradually introduce into your training are specific to a part of the body, there is an overall formula, *"I am calmness throughout,"* that is interspersed throughout the repetition of the other formulae. When you use this formula, the mental contact is made with the body as a whole, possibly by feeling as if you are in a "central core" of the body, or as if you are up above the body and looking down and watching it relax.

The First Standard Exercise—Heaviness: The induction of a feeling of heaviness in the limbs has been shown to be particularly conducive to overall relaxation. This exercise is carried out by the use of the following formula, repeated in a *steady filmlike flow* while maintaining *mental contact* with each part. The formulae are, "My right arm is heavy," "My left arm is heavy," "Both legs are heavy," and then finally, "My arms and legs are heavy." These should not always be repeated in the same sequence. Feel free to mix up the order of phrases in random fashion. Remember occasionally (possibly after 3 or 4 other repetitions) to intersperse the phrase "I am calmness throughout" while returning mental contact to your overall body and person. After a period of practicing the above formulae, many people find that they gain a result relatively quickly by simply using the formula, "My arms and legs are heavy." But certainly in the initial stages it is worthwhile to use all of the formulae.

The Second Standard Exercise—Warmth: Just as with heaviness, the induction of warmth in most body parts induces a relaxation effect. The same formulae that were used in the first standard exercise of heaviness are repeated again here. Instead of using the word "heavy," the word "warm" is substituted. During the initial training these are interspersed with the formulae on heaviness so that you might be saying something like, "My right arm is heavy," "My right arm is warm," "My left arm is heavy," "My right arm is warm," etc. As you feel comfortable and relaxed with this, you can experiment with collapsing some of these formulae by using phrases such as "My right arm is heavy and warm," or even going to simply imagining, "Both arms are heavy and warm."

The Third Standard Exercise—Respiration: Allowing oneself to breathe *naturally* is an important step in achieving positive results. Note that you are not necessarily trying to achieve a slow and deep breathing pattern during the exercises. The important thing is letting the breathing eventually take over at its own rate. Thus, the phrase used here is *"My breathing just naturally happens."* This is to emphasize that breathing happens regardless of an individual conscious control.

Passive concentration is especially important here, even though most trainees find it initially difficult to avoid *trying* to breathe slowly and deeply. However, the goal is just to let it happen. The mental contact in this exercise is usually with the general chest area, although some people find it helpful to make mental contact with the overall body. The choice depends on which seems to work most easily for you.

The Fourth Standard Exercise—Abdominal Warmth: The phrase used in this exercise is *"My solar plexus is warm."* The mental contact for this exercise is with that area approximately 2 to 3 inches below the navel. Attainment of warmth in this area effectively counteracts internal disruption from anxiety. Many people find it difficult at first to visualize this area and to gain mental contact with it, but over a period of time they usually feel more comfortable with it. Substituting the phrase "belly" for "solar plexus" in the above formula has been helpful for some people.

The Fifth Standard Exercise—The Cooling of the Forehead: Whereas warmth is conducive to relaxation throughout most parts of the body, the induction of a sense of coolness is most helpful when focusing on the forehead. Thus, the term used in this exercise is *'My forehead is cool and smooth."* The mental contact here is usually made with an overall area an inch or so above the eyes and up into the scalp.

In all of these exercises, you may occasionally note transient images that are related to the effect desired. For example, as regards cooling of the forehead, you may fleetingly envision a cool breeze passing over the forehead, or when speaking of "My legs are warm," you may think of being in a warm bathtub. Such images can be helpful if they are not allowed to continue very long and thus disrupt either the mental contact with the next formula or the steady flow of the formulae.

Most people find it helpful to practice Autogenic Training for a week or two prior to actually getting into Imagery Rehearsal, as this allows a relaxation response to begin to develop. If one is still confused about AT (or somehow distressed with the practice of it), one could 1) consult any of the various books on the subject by Wolfgang Luthe, 2) try an alternative technique such as Jacobson's (1964) "Progressive Relaxation," and 3) consult with a qualified psychologist (one who is state licensed and certified by The American Board of Professional Psychology) who could offer advice or at least a competent referral to a professional who has experience in sports psychology.

*Play softball! for you know not
whence you came, nor why:
Play softball! for you know not
why you go, nor where.*
Edward Fitzgerald
(1809-1883)
*The Rubaiyat of
Omar Khayyam*

Hypnosis

The foregoing techniques can be facilitated by two additional methods, hypnosis and biofeedback. Hypnosis is particularly effective in facilitating Imagery Rehearsal (IR) in individuals who are somehow blocked when trying to do it themselves. For example, an application of hypnosis in this fashion is described by Maurie Pressman in an article entitled "Psychological Techniques for the Advancement of Sports Potential" (Suinn, 1980). He describes several situations in which hypnosis not only facilitated IR, but also allowed these athletes the realization of various deeper conflicts that were decreasing their performance.

Pressman describes the case of a well-known skier who had difficulties reaching any deep level of hypnotic trance. Whenever this skier started to go into a very deep state of hypnosis, he would develop a sensation of falling dangerously. He began to more clearly recall the fear sensations in several early experiences in which he received severe injuries while skiing. But then through the mental associations in hypnosis he came to realize that even more important to the blocking was a strong fear of allowing others, such as coaches and skiing teammates, to have any real control in his world. As he came to realize the negative effect on his performance from these feelings, his skiing substantially improved. This in turn allowed him to go deeper into hypnosis, which then facilitated the Imagery Rehearsal.

Yet, hypnosis is not really a magical technique; it is simply a method for increasing both suggestibility and concentration. It is especially useful (if administered by a licensed psychologist with experience in it) where there is a problem in developing relaxation or when some substantial psychological block is interfering with either effective performance or enjoyment of the sport.

Biofeedback

Biofeedback is a technique in which a person gains an increased awareness of their physiological conditions through technology. For example, if you press your finger on your wrist to hear your pulse, you have instituted a biofeedback system. On the other hand, you don't have the ability to do that with most muscle groups. Thus, a machine to assess the condition of the muscles (EMG) can provide feedback in a more simplified form so that it can be quickly processed. This feedback allows people to change the conditions as they become more and more aware of them. Biofeedback has been used for a variety of psychological and physiological disorders (Meyer, 1983), and since muscle training feedback (EMG) has been one of the most efficient approaches, it can be useful in facilitating athletic performance as well.

As with hypnosis, biofeedback should be used only in conjunction with a qualified professional. Of course, it is unlikely that it would be necessary to use these techniques to increase performance in softball. But it might be helpful for those people in a notably competitive level of softball, or any other sport for that matter.

This maiden she lived with no other thought
Than to love and to play softball with me.
 Edgar Allan Poe
 (1809-1849)
 Annabel Lee (1849)

Defusing Thoughts

An additional psychological technique for improving performance in sports is termed *Defusing Thoughts.* Persistant distracting thoughts about performance often interfere with athletes in various sports (Nideffer, 1981; Cratty, 1983). For example, thoughts like "I just can't make another error," or "If I don't start getting some hits, I'll be sitting on the bench" not only disrupt concentration on the game itself, but they set up a number of physiological reactions which impair performance as well.

First off, they elicit a version of the "fight or flight" reaction. The fight-or-flight reaction to such thoughts is an automatic emotional response generated in the hypothalamus, a walnut-size portion of the brain that acts as a central switchboard for various physiological functions. The hypothalamus releases a hormone that activates the pituitary gland, which in term sets up a cycle that releases several other hormones, namely cortisone, epinephrine, norepinephrine, and especially adrenalin. In small bursts, this reaction can be channeled into an effective performance.

However, it's more common for the body to overreact (Mirkin and Hoffman, 1978). The muscles tense up, the digestive system closes down (often producing nausea) and the bronchial tubes even tend to tighten up, creating shallower and faster breathing, a "choking" in both the literal and figurative sense. Psychologically, anxiety is cued by these physiological reactions, and this is added to the anxiety already experienced in anticipating possible failure. So a vicious cycle is set up in which anticipated failure or other threats set off physiological reactions, which in turn impair physical performance and set off further anxiety.

Certainly, the approaches of Autogenic Relaxation training and Imagery Rehearsal, described earlier in this book, are useful as preventive techniques for such situations. Another method that has been helpful is to consciously use a "Defusing Thought" to block a negative thinking pattern. Examples of relevant defusing thoughts for the prior concerns are respectively "Errors happen, and even if I had another one, that would not be the best situation, but it would be alright," and "It's silly to think that I suddenly lost the ability to hit well. I'll just hit away and focus on doing the hitting right and the hits will come." If the negative thoughts are truly persistent, the Defusing Thought can be introduced into Autogenic Training to be repeated as one of the formulae. This seems to enhance the effect.

If the negative thought is a rather diffuse but persistent and destructive one, such as "I'm really no good in sports anyway, and I don't know why I even come and play softball," or something like that, the appropriate defusing thought would be "I may not be the best at this game, but I can and do enjoy it and I do have fun with my friends when I do so." This also can be introduced into Autogenic Training, and in addition, should be occasionally repeated in ordinary life situations by use of the Premack Principle.

The Premack Principle holds that a higher probability behavior reinforces a lower probability behavior. What this means is that if one tags the newly desired behavior (the defusing thought) on to a behavior that is highly probable (picking one's wallet up off the dresser, putting the key into the car to start it, etc.), the newly desired behavior or thought will become more common and effective. The first step is to purposefully start saying the defusing thought on these high probability occasions. As this continues, the new thought becomes more common in thinking, more influential in thinking and behavior, and the constant reinforcement by the high probability behavior becomes less necessary.

While the above are useful techniques in the ongoing or long-term preparation for softball, or most other sports, let's now consider some methods that are useful immediately before playing a game.

Immediate Preparation

Estragon: Let's go.
Vladimir: We can't.
Estragon: Why not?
Vladimir: We're waiting for the game to start.
  Samuel Beckett
  (1906-   )
  Waiting for Godot

While the preceeding techniques are geared more toward a long-term preparation for playing the game better, the techniques described in this section are most useful at the time of the game itself. The major psychological method described, reflecting the work of Tutko (1976) as well as that of Nideffer (1981) and Cratty (1983), is an analysis of various psych-out techniques, along with some comments on how to cope with them. Simple recognition of the opponent's psych-out technique is itself a major step toward elimination of any disruptive effect.

The physical technique suggested is a modern approach to loosening up by stretching, primarily following upon the work of Bob Anderson (1980). These exercises not only serve to reduce injuries, but they generate a muscular "looseness" and a psychological relaxation, both of which facilitate better play.

"Do other men, for they would do you."
That's the true softball precept.
  Charles Dickens
  (1812-1870)
  Martin Chuzzlewit

Psychological Techniques
Effective athletes stay aware of the fact that the other team or individuals on that team may resort to "psych-outs." Through psychological means

The simple recognition of the opponent's psyche-out technique is itself a major step toward elimination of any disruptive effect.

they attempt to introduce a distraction into their opponent's performance. As Tutko (1976) has pointed out, psych-outs generally fall into four major categories: Provocation, Evoking guilt feelings, Intimidation, and Distraction. In actuality, they all ultimately function effectively to the degree that they are "distractions."

Twinkle, twinkle, little bat
How I wonder what you're at
Up above the world you fly
When I throw you in the sky.
> Lewis Carroll
> (1832-1898)
> *Alice's Adventures in*
> *Wonderland*

Provocation

There are several "games" under the category of provocation that can be used to psych-out an opponent. A common technique in team sports is *Taunting*. This is a rather unsophisticated technique in which the abilities of the other player or team are derided by such comments as "You don't honestly think you can hit the ball standing like that," or "Aren't you embarrassed to always make an out," or "Hey, great catch, fella" after someone has made an error.

A more sophisticated technique can be *Ignoring Lesser Mortals*. In this technique, one simply, but in an obvious manner, ignores the achievements of the other team or player. This, however, is usually effective only in individual competitions, since the ignoring of another player in team sports is compensated for by the support of their own team. Even in individual competitions, it is primarily effective only with young players or players still overdependent on recognition from their opponent, especially if that opponent is in any way one of their heroes.

A pushing lady: 'What are your views on love?'
Mme. Leroi: 'Love? I make it constantly
but never talk about it.'
> Marcel Proust
> (1871-1922)
> *Le Côté de Guermantes*

A third subcategory in this area is that of *Expert Advice*. Comments such as "I think you could get more power in your swing if you stood with your legs farther apart" or "That was a nice hit you made last time up, but I think you can get more power into it if you would hold the bat farther down toward the end," are typical. It can be especially upsetting to certain players when the psych-out artist adds condescension, such as in "I'll just throw it right in there easy and give you a good shot at it."

The first blow is half the battle.
Oliver Goldsmith
(1730-1774)
She Stoops to Conquer

Intimidation

Techniques such as the *Slam-dunk* come under the category of intimidation. Though the term "slam-dunk" refers to a play in basketball, in which the ball is forced through the basket with immense power, it offers such a graphic description of the technique that it is worth using here. One softballer whom I have played with in the past always likes to try to rap one hard line drive toward the bench of the opposing team early in the game. This does upset the people on the bench, and it is his belief that this carries over to some of his opponents on the field. An especially hard slide into base is a variation on this approach.

A second form of intimidation can be referred to as the *Secret Method.* In this approach, a player implies that special training or a special bat is available that gives an advantage over the other players. It usually takes a real con-man to carry this off with confidence, but it can be quite effective.

Evoking Guilt Feelings

Under the category of evoking guilt feelings are techniques like the *Friendly Opponent* and the *Weak Opponent.* The Friendly Opponent is always ready to congratulate you after you make a good play, often implying that everyone naturally expects a continuation of that level of performance. Players often like to combine this with the Weak Opponent approach in which they suggest they really don't belong on the same field with you, or that their team unfortunately was put in a tougher league than they should have been, or some similar approach. Variations of this technique emphasize physical or psychological excuses for predicted poor performance, or messages that there really isn't much interest in the competitive aspects of the game anyway. If this approach is taken seriously by an opponent, it may quickly sap both concentration and motivation.

Distraction

The fourth category, distraction, has several subcategories. In fact, distraction is at least one goal in virtually all techniques, even those already described. Any technique that ultimately distracts from concentration on performance is likely to ultimately reduce effectiveness (Nideffer, 1981). Some distraction approaches are close to that of the Friendly Opponent, in that comments are made like "Man, when you move your foot back like that you really can pull that ball like a rocket—I'm glad I don't play third base." If players pay much attention to such comments, they soon find themselves practically stepping back into the dugout in order to rip the ball with such admired ferocity. They may hit some hard foul balls and a rare fair hit. But, they are more than likely to start popping the ball up or to hit feeble grounders because of the loss of concentration.

Blowing Up, various forms of temper tantrums, are often useful as distracters. Several noted baseball managers, such as Earl Weaver and Billy Martin, were famous for using this technique to fire up their team or to interrupt the game when the other team seemed to be getting into the rhythm of their performance.

In another type of distraction method, there is an attempt to get the athlete to notice *Extraneous Factors,* as in comments like "Boy, that's really a short fence out in left field" or "These damn balls they use here are so soft you never can really get a big hit anymore." The more players pay attention to such quotes, the more their concentration and motivation is disrupted.

The one means that wins the easiest victory over reason: terror and force.
   Adolf Hitler
   (1889-1945)
   Mein Kampf

Responding to Psych-Outs

There are several ways to deal with psych-outs. The major way to gain some awareness of these games is to continually and persistently observe them whenever they occur. It's surprising but true that simple awareness dilutes the potency of these techniques to the point where they become absurd enough to be laughable. One can proceed to point out to the perpetrator the absurdity of the game being used, and even laugh at the game and then let it go. But the danger here is getting into a contest as to who can psych-out who, and this in itself can be distracting. The best approach is to combine an increased awareness of the game with a rededication to concentrating on one's own performance, and avoiding attending to what others are doing. For example, clearly remind yourself that your focus needs to be on your own physical and psychological state and your standard preparation for the game. At the same time, one need not be a complete ass in this regard. It's reasonable to accept praise in a pleased but relatively disinterested fashion. Also, a simple agreement with many of the comments described earlier makes further attempts at distraction often seem silly to the perpetrator.

Let's now turn to some physical techniques that are useful in a pre-game preparation.

Softball is one percent inspiration and ninety-nine percent perspiration.
Thomas Alva Edison
(1847-1931)
Life

Physical Techniques

In addition to being properly conditioned for softball through the techniques noted in the section on general preparation, most players find it very helpful to spend some time loosening up immediately prior to a game. Most athletes are aware that such pre-game preparation prevents muscle strains or worse injuries. But in addition, loosening up also fosters a better performance as well, since it decreases tension and anxiety and increases overall reaction time.

Since the major demands in a softball game come from throwing, fielding, running, and swinging a bat, it is these four specific activities for which one should especially loosen up. Most softball players do spend a considerable time throwing before the game. In contrast they usually spend little time loosening up for batting, fielding, or running.

The length of time that one needs to spend loosening up is primarily related to three factors: temperature, age, and physical condition. Certainly, the last two variables, age and physical condition, are highly correlated, though there are plenty of examples of young athletes who are in horrible condition, and older athletes who are in good physical condition. Nevertheless, the general rule is that the older athletes are, the worse physical condition they are in, and the more time needs to be spent on loosening up.

Mad dogs, Englishmen, and soft-ballers go out in the mid-day sun.
Noel Coward
(1899-1973)
Mad Dogs and Englishmen

At certain times, the most critical variable is temperature. In the early weeks of spring, as softball leagues gear up again, or in the tapering off season of fall leagues, the air can be quite cool, especially for night games. More preparation is needed at these times, not only to prevent muscle pulls, but also simply to perform at peak effectiveness. A loosening up process is very useful during the early spring months. Not only is there the coolness in many locales throughout the country, but, in addition, the body has not yet become used to the singular demands of softball, so specific muscles are more easily strained.

The type of game one will be playing in is another factor. When you're playing for the championship of the city league, you're going to go all out on every hit and dive for grounders that you might let go in a Saturday afternoon beer game. So it's worthwhile to assess how vigorously one will probably participate in a game, and if it's likely to be strenuous, more time for loosening up should be allowed.

At the same time, some athletes get so caught up and obsessed with warm-ups that they get beyond the peak of performance and fatigue starts to set in. From what I've seen, this is seldom a risk with softball players. However, there are always a few people in any situation who overdo a good thing. This is especially likely to take its toll in the later innings, just at the point when players need that extra burst of energy.

While most athletes recognize the value of loosening up, this is usually thought of only as a process to be engaged in before the game. Yet, in many instances, periodic loosening up throughout the game is worthwhile, especially if the player has not been very active in that particular game. Periodic "re-warming-up" is specially advantageous for those players who don't enter the game until the later innings.

It is better to wear out than rust out.
Bishop Richard Cumberland
(1841-1929)
G. Horne's *The Duty of*
Contending for the Faith

Stretching Exercises

The principal recommended method for loosening up prior to a game is the use of static stretching exercises. Essentially there are two kinds of stretching exercises, *ballistic* and *static.* Ballistic exercises are the type that most people think of when they consider warming up for athletic events. Ballistic exercises are "bounce-type" exercises, toe touches, for instance, in which the muscles are rapidly extended and then almost just as quickly brought back into place. Though most people think they are warming up with these exercises, ballistic stretching exercises cause a high rate of contraction in what are actually cold muscles. Ballistic type exercises can be useful in strengthening muscles, but only if these muscles have already been warmed up. If they have not been warmed up, there is a substantial risk of putting too much stress on the ligaments and tendons, which can easily be torn since they are nonelastic. If this type of injury, or any other type of sports related injury does occur, recourse to a physician with a specific interest in sports medicine is recommended. A list of such physicians in any locale can be obtained from the American Orthopaedic Society for Sports Medicine, 430 N. Michigan Ave., Chicago, Ill., 60611.

Static stretching exercises, however, help to prevent injuries by both emphasizing slowness in reaching the position and also keeping that position for a significant period of time in a relatively relaxed fashion. Since the action is slow, the stress in the stretch becomes focused on the center of the muscle, rather than the ends of the muscle where damage can be done to tendons and ligaments.

There does seem to be a bias in our culture against static exercises. They have primarily been viewed in Western culture only as a type of yoga. Those of us from Western cultures also seem to often feel that if exercises don't make us sweat and hurt they probably are not really helpful. But since static exercises do not involve violent contractions and contortions, they actually warm the muscles by slowly unsheathing them, which allows blood in, as well as it's accompanying oxygen. Overall, static exercises increase circulation of fresh blood, remove waste products from the muscles, and help with healing.

In addition, static stretching exercises actually strengthen the muscles as well as warm them up (a fact that is surprising to many American coaches). This static stretching makes the muscles more flexible, which in turn increases their efficient strength. Efficient muscle strength is determined by the distance over which the muscles are able to contract. So if increased flexibility is obtained by these static stretching exercises, there is a greater distance for the muscle to contract as it lengthens. When it then does contract, more strength is generated for an action such as swinging a bat, throwing a ball, or stretching for a catch.

In addition to both warming and strengthening the muscles, static stretching exercises also provide a relaxation effect which facilitates the overall concentration on the game itself. During the exercises, it is advised that while the stretch is being held, the person exercising also pay attention to breathing rate, not trying to change it one way or another, but simply attending to it. Such focused attention provides a relaxation and calming effect, and in addition increases the ability to concentrate on various aspects of the game itself. Some people also find that it's helpful to run through some Imagery Rehearsal exercises (described earlier in this book) while doing the stretching exercises. This increases the potency of both the physical stretching exercises and the Imagery Rehearsal. Since the stretching is slow, you should not experience any significant pain or distress, but if you do, stop the exercises and seek expert advice.

The following static stretching exercises are especially suited for softball or baseball. Several of them are adapted from Bob Anderson's excellent book, *Stretching* (1980), published by Shelter Publications and distributed by Random House. Pat Croce's book, *Stretching for Athletics* (1983), also offers some very fine stretching routines that are specifically applicable to a variety of sports.

Specific Stretching Exercises for Softball

Exercise #1. In this exercise, you should stand up and raise your hands directly over your head in a relaxed Y configuration. Then gradually stretch upward and outward trying to exert a stretching all throughout the muscles of your upper body. In essence, pull yourself up and out, feeling the pull throughout your chest and back as well as your arms and even your fingers. Gradually attain as full a stretch as possible and then hold this stretch for approximately 12 seconds. Do this once as you lift your heels up and move up onto your toes. Then do it a second time as you pull your toes up while tilting back on your heels. You may also add to this exercise by opening your mouth and giving a "silent shout." This provides the benefit of stretching to the facial and throat muscles. These latter stretches are, of course, not particularly critical to softball (unless you are preparing to do a lot of hollering and complaining), but they are helpful overall physiologically. You can do an effective variant on this exercise by performing it in the prone position, e.g., while lying on a bed, the floor or the ground.

Exercise #2. Move from the *Exercise #1* into a position wherein your hands are straight over your head. Then bend them from the elbow into a position so tht the fingers of the left hand are touching the outer side of the elbow of the right arm. Then, with your knees slightly bent, gradually stretch from the waist toward your left side; now grasp your right elbow with your left hand and pull with a gentle stretch directly across the top of your head. Move into a comfortable but moderately tense stretch, and hold this for 10-12 seconds. Reverse all the positions with the hands, and do this to the right side.

Exercise #3. While standing with your right side next to a wall or a chain link fence, reach *back* with your right hand at shoulder level and grasp the fence or wall. Now bring your left arm around and behind your back at approximately belt level. You can either push this arm as far as it will go around your back or reach out and back and grasp the fence with it. At the same time, look over your left shoulder back toward your right hand which is holding onto the fence. Move so that you feel the stretch in your upper right arm and shoulders as much as is comfortably feasible, and then hold this approximately 10-12 seconds. Now, move your right hand and arm further up the chain link fence or wall, approximately another foot up, and go through the exercise again in the same fashion you just did. Then, reverse the procedure now working through these two exercises with the left hand on the wall or fence.

Exercise #4. To stretch your calf muscles, ankle joint and your Achilles tendon, first stand approximately a foot or so away from this same fence and lean forward with your hands on it and with your head resting on your hands. Put one leg straight behind you as you move the other into a knee bend. Your back (or straight leg) and your upper body should form a triangle with the wall or fence and the ground. Move your hips forward keeping this straight line. Keep the heel of the back leg, the one kept straight, on the ground, with the toes pointed directly ahead or even slightly turned in. Move into a easy stretch that you feel in the back calf muscles and in the front of the ankle. Hold for 25 to 30 seconds without bouncing or moving. Now move from this straight line body position by simply bending the back leg slightly. This should exert a stretch in the area slightly below the calf muscles, focusing on the Achilles tendon. Do not exert a substantial stretch here, but make it comfortable as you bend your knee forward, again keeping the heel down. Hold this stretch without strain for approximately 25 to 30 seconds. Now, simply reverse the positions to exercise the same muscles in the other leg.

Exercise #5. Since softball emphasizes a shifting of the weight quickly back and forth across the thighs, hips, and lower back, this exercise is especially helpful, as it is for other games that also use this shift (tennis, basketball, etc.). First, put your feet together, and bend your knees such that your legs are at a 45 degree angle with the plane of your hips, that is, you go halfway down to an apparent sitting position. As you do, push out your butt as if preparing to sit down on a chair. Clasp your knees by putting your hands on the front part of each knee and keep your eyes straight ahead. Now, first moving from left to right, try to rotate your buttocks in a circle about the size of a volleyball. Then simply reverse the motion from right to left. You may feel a bit absurd in doing this exercise. However, you should note a comfortable loosening in the hips and upper thigh areas. Please note that this is the only exercise that does not involve holding a static stretch. But, performed slowly and with as fluid a movement as possible, it generates a positive physiological effect throughout the body.

**Orandum est ut sit meus sana
in corpore sano.
You should pray to have a
sound mind in a sound body.**
Juvenal
(60-130 A.D.)
Satires

Exercise #6. In order to stretch the front thigh muscles (quadriceps), as well as some of the muscles of the lower leg, reach behind with your right arm and grasp your left leg by the toes as you bring it up behind you. You may find it necessary to balance against a fence while doing this one. Take the top of your left foot with your right hand and stretch your leg up and back toward your butt. Slowly move into a comfortable stretch position and hold this for approximately 25 seconds. Then simply reverse the position. If you have no fence available and have difficulty retaining your balance, this can be done while lying down flat on your stomach.

Exercise #7. This exercise is designed to stretch the important hamstrings in the legs, often a site of injuries in softball. It is more effective if you have first stretched the quadriceps before stretching the hamstrings, so always do this exercise after the previous one. Sit down on the ground with your right leg stretched out at a 45 degree angle. Bring your left foot up in toward your groin area so that the knee is bent and the sole of your foot is as flat as possible against your upper inner thigh. Now, slowly reach forward from the hips down toward your right foot with both hands. Move your upper body forward to a position where you feel at least a slight stretch, but do not strain in this movement. First, hold this position for about 15 to 20 seconds. Then slowly just move your upper body and arms a bit more forward, and hold this position for approximately 25 seconds, again without causing any pain or excessive strain. Make sure that you keep your right foot pointing straight up in the air, with the toes and ankles generally relaxed. Also, be sure that the muscles on the top front area of your thighs, the quadriceps, are reasonably relaxed and thus somewhat soft to the touch. Keep your head upright during the stretch. Now, simply reverse this position and do the stretch on your left side.

Exercise #8. Moving from the prior position, simply lay back and put your hands on your chest. With your knees bent, try to bring the soles of your feet together and then bring your feet up toward your body but as flat as possible on the ground, allowing your legs to spread out. Hold this comfortable stretch position for approximately 25 to 30 seconds. then gradually and gently rock your legs back and forth, moving your knees only approximately an inch in rotation in order to feel a movement in your hips and groin area.

Exercise #9. Lay your head back flat, and bring your knees together while bent so that they are pointing directly up in the air. The soles of your feet are kept on the ground, with the feet relatively close together. Now, reach back behind your neck with your hands and interlock your fingers. Gradually move your head up and forward toward your chest, gently pulling with your hands until you feel a comfortable stretch in your head and neck area. Hold this position for approximately 10-12 seconds. Return to the original position, with your head on the ground; then do this stretch again two more times.

Exercise #10. While prone and keeping your head back as in the prior position, put your legs both flat and pointing out and down from your body. Reach down and grasp your right knee at the front of the knee as you bring it up toward your chest. Keep the lower part of your leg on a plane parallel with the ground, and do not begin to point it upward. Keep the toes pointed out and down in a relatively flat plane and pull the leg in toward the chest so that you feel a stretch in the muscles of the back and in the back of the leg. Keep your back flat through this exercise. Hold this position for approximately 25 to 30 seconds. Now, from this position, gradually pull your knee toward your opposite shoulder, exerting pull across your chest. This should create a stretch on the outside of your right hip if you are pulling your right leg up. Hold this position, emphasizing a gentle stretch on the outside of the leg and hips for about 20 to 25 seconds. Then simply reverse the exercise to stretch the other side.

Exercise #11. Move into a standing position with your knees straight but not locked. The muscles and joints should not be tense. Place your feet approximately a foot apart and then extend your arms in front of you with your palms downward. Now arch your spine and extend your butt out behind you, pushing back toward your butt as it extends backward. Exhale and then bend down and try to touch the ground with the palms of your hands. The point here is to *try* to touch the ground. You will not likely be able to do this at first. Don't drop your head forward, but move down toward the ground with your hands straight out until you feel the stretch, and hold this for approximately 15 seconds. It is helpful in this exercise to take a visual fix with your eyes on some point in front of you, after you have arched your spine. Try to keep in eye contact with that point as you move your palms down toward the ground.

Exercise #12. Slowly, and in sequence, grasp each finger with the opposite hand, and gently and deliberately but firmly stretch the finger up and back while holding the other fingers forward and together. Stretch the finger as far as you can without pain, and hold the position for approximately 20 seconds. After you have stretched each finger and thumb, slowly bend all fingers into a fist, without pain, and hold for 10 seconds, release, and wiggle the fingers for 5 seconds or so.

Exercise #13. Simply repeat *Exercise #1.* again, emphasizing a slow and gentle stretching of all the muscles, especially feeling the stretch throughout your fingers and wrists and in your upper chest and back area. Hold this for approximately 20 to 25 seconds. Then relax, breathe deeply, and repeat this once more.

Softball is the only thing that can go on mattering once it has stopped hurting.
Elizabeth Bowen
(1899-1973)
The Heat of the Day

Throughout all of these exercises, please keep in mind that you are never to stretch to a point of pain. Rather, seek a gentle stretch that you can gradually increase as you practice these exercises over time. Focus on your breathing as you do the stretching, allowing it to become slow and regular. At the same time think about the area being stretched and experience that stretch, though never to the point of strain. Slowly reach the stretch and hold it.

It is very helpful if you can also practice these stretching exercises at times other than just before a game, as this will significantly increase your flexibility. Both Anderson's and Croce's books offer a great many more stretching exercises than the ones listed above, and it is useful to pratice a variety of these at times other than just before a game. The particular set above is especially helpful for game preparation, but you will not find much gain in flexibility if this is the only time you do stretching exercises (unless you are a true softball addict and play four or more times a week).

After completing your stretching exercises, it's worthwhile to do some running. Many of the needs for loosening up would be taken care of if players would spend a bit more time running before the game. Running puts a degree of stress on most of the important muscles used in softball, particularly in the upper leg muscles, such as the quadriceps, but also in the hamstrings. In particular, many injuries in sports, including in softball, involve a pulled hamstring. A substantial number of these could be prevented by more emphasis on running during a warm-up period, first slowly, and then more quickly. If you would like more information on running, there are a variety of informative running magazines available, or you can consult the original definitive book on this topic—*The Complete Book of Running* by James Fixx (1977).

When you run as a part of your loosening up process, emphasize starting with a gentle jogging pace and then eventually move into a full sprint as you feel warmed up and comfortable. Focus on eliminating any tensions by not making a fist as you run, and think looseness in your shoulders and the upper back region where tension often resides. Others have found that they run relaxed if they concentrate on allowing relaxation in the tongue or in the anal area, thus the odd motto "Run with an open asshole."

Also, focus on allowing a natural rhythm to develop both in your running and in your breathing. One way to do this is to consciously focus on lifting one knee while "grabbing" the ground with your other foot and toes, and then pushing off. Start doing this in a jogging pattern, and then as your concentration effectively focuses on this pace, move into a faster run and then a sprint, always keeping your consciousness on the pattern. Keep running until you feel comfortable and relaxed, and your muscles are loose and warmed up. Finish up with the first stretching exercise noted earlier, as well as other stretches that seem as if they would be helpful in eliminating any tenseness that remains.

Now that you have completed the stretching exercises and some running, go through all of the movements that are typically used in the game. Do some throwing, swing the bat a few times, and field some balls. By this point, you should be relaxed and comfortable physically, without any of the undue tension that can lead to a poor performance, or even worse, to injuries.

In order to have your practice facilitate game performance, try to simulate conditions as exactly as possible. For example, if you are a

Julie Martin reminds us that when all is said and done, the game is meant to be fun.
Photo courtesy of ASA

pitcher, don't just keep throwing practice pitches to your catcher in a very quick back and forth exchange, as this is dissimilar to game conditions. Instead, take a moment before each pitch, consider an imaginary batter preparing to hit your pitch, and then try to pitch with the same mental attitude you would have when facing a real batter. Similarly, when participating in an infield or outfield warmup, do so from the position you usually take in the field. Pretend that there is an imaginary runner so that your throws and other movements will be as close as possible to game conditions.

If you follow a significant proportion of the suggestions, you should play better softball, and you will probably get more enjoyment out of the game as well.

God obligeth no man to more than he hath given him ability to perform.
The Koran

After all, tomorrow is another day for softball.
Margaret Mitchell
(1900-1949)
Gone With the Wind (1936)

4

Appendices

Softball Terms Worth Knowing

Know then Thyself, presume not God to scan
The proper study of mankind is softball.
Alexander Pope
(1688-1744)
Essay on Man

ALTERED BAT: An altered bat is one that has its physical structure changed, thus rendering it illegal for use. Examples of altering a bat are inserting lead at the end of the bat or replacing the handle of a metal bat with a wooden handle. It is not illegal and thus considered to be altering the bat to replace the grip with another legal grip.

APPEAL PLAY: An appeal play is one in which there is a request to the umpire to change his opinion, based on a rule violation. The four major appeal plays are (1) leaving a base before a fly ball is touched or caught; (2) touching a base out of order or not touching the base at all; (3) overrunning first base and then being tagged while attempting to go to second; (4) batting out of order. The appeal must be made before the next pitch or before the defensive team leaves the field.

ASSIST: This is an officially scored fielding credit that goes to the player who helps another teammate make a putout. If that teammate subsequently makes an error resulting in an inability to make the putout, the assist is still credited to the first player.

BACKING UP: Playing behind a teammates in order to retrieve the ball in case he misses it.

BACK STOP: This refers to the fence behind the plate, though in some instances it may be applied to the catcher as a nickname.

BALK: An illegal move in pitching which encourages the runners to advance a base, the penalty for which is that the runners are allowed to advance to that base.

BASE ON BALLS: This occurs when the pitcher runs up four pitches judged by the umpire to be out of the strike zone, thus called "balls." The batter is allowed to advance to first base without being put out; also termed a "walk."

BASE PATH: The base path, sometimes termed a base line, is an imaginary path 3 feet wide on each side of a direct line between the bases. In theory, a runner who moves outside of this lane can be called out, unless he is trying to avoid a fielder in the process of making a play. In actuality, being called out for stepping out of the base path is uncommon.

BASE RUNNER: A base runner is a player on the team at bat who is either on first, second, or third base and who has not been yet put out.

BATTER'S BOX: The legal area in which the person preparing to bat the ball, referred to as the batter, must stand (seldom enforced in most leagues).

BATTERY: The pitcher and the catcher.

BATTING AVERAGE: A player's total number of hits in a league or season divided by the number of times at bat, usually expressed in a three decimal number such a .300. Walks, sacrifice hits, and free bases are not considered as times at bat in figuring out the batting average, though errors are included as outs.

BATTING ORDER: Officially listed sequence in which the players on a team will bat. Batting out of the order of this list will result in a player being called out if detected.

BEAT OUT: To beat an infielder's throw to first base and thus get a hit—on a ball that has been cleanly fielded.

BEHIND ON THE COUNT: If there have been more strikes than balls called, the batter is "behind on the count"; if more balls than strikes, then the pitcher is behind.

BLOCKED BALL: A thrown or batted ball that is touched or stopped by a person not in the game, or a ball that touches something that is not part of the official equipment on the field, becomes a dead ball. Play is usually stopped at that point.

BLOOPER: A short fly ball that just drops over the infielder for a base hit. It is not usually produced intentionally.

BOBBLE: Juggling or dropping the ball while attempting to catch it.

BOTTOM: The second part of an inning. The first team to come to bat in any inning is said to be batting in the top of the inning, the second team in the bottom.

BOX SCORE: A tally of all important events in the game, such as the number of runs, hits, and errors, usually kept as a series of symbols.

BUNT: A ball that is lightly tapped by the batter so that it rolls slowly to the infield. It is illegal in slow-pitch softball so the batter is called out and the runners have to return to their original bases.

CATCH: A catch of the ball is made legally with the hands or glove. A ball that is held up by the player's body or clothing is not a legal catch until it moves to the glove or hand without touching the ground. The player must have had some control of the ball for even a brief moment in order for it to be a valid catch.

CATCHER'S BOX: Legally designated area in which the catcher may stand while receiving a pitch. In actuality, the catcher is often allowed to move out of this area in order to avoid being hit with the bat.

CHOKE: Misplay(s) from excessive apprehension or physical tension. The bronchial tubes constrict during severe anxiety, causing an actual though mild choking sensation.

CHOKE UP: Gripping the bat closer to the hitting area of the bat in order to gain more control of the bat.

CHOPPED BALL: The batter strikes downward with a chopping motion of the bat usually causing the ball to bounce very high, thus allowing the runner to beat the throw to first. It is illegal in slow-pitch softball and the batter is declared out and runners must return to their original bases

CLEAN-UP: The fourth position in the batting order, usually given to the person who is the most consistent home run hitter.

COACH: A member of the team at bat who directs the players on the bases from the coaching boxes next to first and third base. Two coaches are allowed.

CORNER: A part of home plate: "the inside corner" is a small portion of the plate closest to the batter; "the outside corner" being the part of the plate farthest away from the batter.

COUNT: The number of balls and strikes on the person at bat. A count of "3 and 2" indicates that there are three balls and two strikes on the batter.

CROWDING THE PLATE: When a batter stands very close to the plate, occasionally leaning over it.

CUT: To swing at a pitched ball; as in the term "good cut," meaning a hard swing.

CUT-OFF: The interception of a ball that is being thrown to another teammate. A cut-off is made in order to try to trap someone running to another base.

DEAD BALL: A ball that is no longer in play. Technically, it is not in play again until the plate umpire has called "play ball," though most umpires don't bother with this and simply wave the game into play again.

DEEP: An offensive player who stands as far away from the pitcher as possible in the batter's box. A defensive player who is playing farther away from the batter than is usual.

DEFENSIVE TEAM: The team on the field.

DISH: Home plate; (2) an attractive player or fan of the opposite sex.

DOUBLE PLAY: A play by the defense in which two offensive players become legally out as result of continuous action, sometimes referred to as a "twin killing."

DRIVE: A hard hit ball.

EARNED RUN: Every runner that reaches home plate by a combination of walks, sacrifices or safe hits. If at any time the runner advanced through an error, it is not an earned run.

EARNED RUN AVERAGE: The number of earned runs a pitcher has allowed divided by the number of innings pitched.

ERROR: A defensive misplay which allows a base runner to reach a base or take an extra base which he should not have been able to take, to remain on a base longer than he should, or to bat longer than he should. A base on balls is not an error.

FAIR BALL: Any legally batted ball that falls *on* or between the first or third base foul lines which extend (unfortunately not very clearly in some cases) from home through the bases down to their right and left field "corners." A ball is fair if it touches any player or umpire in fair territory or passes over any part of fair territory and then goes out into the outfield before going foul.

FAN: (1) a nonparticipant who is watching the game; (2) to swing at the ball and miss it, especially on a third strike.

FIELDER'S CHOICE: A play in which the fielder attempts to put out a base runner rather than the batter going to first base.

FLY BALL: Any ball batted into the air that goes beyond the infield. If it stays within the infield, it is usually referred to as pop-up.

FOOT IN THE BUCKET: To pull away from the ball while batting, usually by taking the forward foot (toward the pitcher) and moving it away from the plate; usually resulting in a ball hit down the line or into foul territory.

FORCED OUT: An out made by touching the next base to which a runner has been forced to advance because there are runners on all bases behind him.

FORFEIT: A game which has been stopped by the umpire and awarded as a win to one of the teams for various reasons such as refusal to continue to play the game by the other team, or starting a fight.

FOUL BALL: A batted ball which goes past first or third base in foul territory, which touches an umpire or player in foul territory, or settles in foul territory after being in the fair area but not going beyond first or third base. A ball which strikes home plate and moves directly into fair territory and stays there is a fair ball.

FOUL LINE: A white line (at least at the start of the season) extending from home plate out over third and first base out to the fences. The foul lines themselves are fair territory—they go at right angles out from home plate.

FOUL TIP: A batted ball that is caught by the catcher. If it does not go higher than the batter's head, it is called a strike; if it does, it is called an out.

FREE TRIP: A base on balls or a walk.

FROZEN ROPE: A line drive hit with such force that it does not appear to have any arc in it.

FULL COUNT: A count of three balls and two strikes against the person who is batting.

FUNGO HITTING: A technique for giving fielding practice in which a player or coach tosses the ball up and bats it in turn to the various fielders.

GRASS CUTTER: A batted ball hit with great force and speed very close to or on the ground.

GROOVE: To pitch the ball squarely in the center of the strike zone, usually considered an easy pitch to hit very hard.

GROUND BALL: A batted ball that bounces or rolls along the ground.

HOLE: When referring to the defense, "hole" refers to an area not covered easily by one of the defensive players. In reference to the offense, it refers to a place in the batting order in which there is a series of weak hitters.

HOME TEAM: The team which bats second, or during "the bottom" of the inning, traditionally the team on whose field the game is played.

HOOK SLIDE: A slide in which the runner goes in feet first and then twists away from the defensive player, while reaching back with the rear foot to hook the edge of the bag with the toe.

HOT CORNER: The third base area, so called because of the high number of hard hit balls that usually go into this area.

ILLEGAL BAT: A bat that does not meet official requirements, such as a baseball bat or an altered bat. Using an illegal bat may result in suspension from the game.

ILLEGALLY BATTED BALL: A ball that is struck by the batter with an illegal bat or while his or her foot is either touching home plate or is completely outside the batter's box. The batter is out, and if an illegal bat is involved, the player may also be suspended from the game.

ILLEGALLY CAUGHT BALL: A ball caught by the clothing, cap, or mask of a player. Base runners are allowed two free bases on a thrown ball, three on a batted ball, and all four if the ball would have made it over the fence without the interference.

INFIELD: The portion of the field generally included in the area bounded by home plate, the bases, and where the infielders play.

INFIELD FLY: A fly ball in fair territory that is easily handled by an infielder. If there are runners on all bases or on first and second and less than two outs, the batter is immediately called out. Runners may advance after it is caught. If a declared infield fly is allowed to fall uncaught to the ground and then bounces foul before passing first and third base, it is a foul ball.

INNING: Each sequential portion of the game during which both teams have a turn at bat.

INTERFERENCE: The act of any offensive player which the umpire has declared has illegally hindered a defensive player's attempt to execute a play. The person interfering is declared out. Interference also occurs if the catcher attempts to prevent the batter from hitting a pitched ball.

KEYSTONE SACK: Second base.

LEAD-OFF: The person who bats first for his team either at the start of the game or the start of an inning. It also can refer to moving off the base before a ball is pitched, though this is illegal in slow-pitch softball.

LEGAL TOUCH: When a runner is touched by the ball which is being held by the defensive player. The ball may be inside the glove of a fielder and not directly touch the runner in order for that person to be out. If the defensive play juggles the ball while making the touch or immediately drops the ball (without declared interference by the runner) there is no out.

LINE DRIVE: A hard hit ball that stays relatively low to the ground, and does not develop a high arc.

MUFF: An error on a hit or thrown ball that should have been easily caught.

OBSTRUCTION: The action of a fielder who, while not actually fielding a batted ball or being in possession of the ball, interferes with the progress of a base runner who is legally running the bases. Generally, that runner is allowed a free base, and all the other runners are allowed to advance one base.

OFFENSIVE TEAM: The team at bat.

ONE-TWO-THREE: When a side makes three outs without any batter reaching first base successfully.

OUTFIELD: That portion of the field beyond the infield area and bounded by the first and third base foul lines.

OVERSLIDE OR OVERRUN: When a runner, usually inadvertently, goes beyond the base that he or she is sliding into or running to. Batter-runners may overslide or overrun first base without being in jeopardy of being tagged out if they do not make a clear move to go on to second base (such as turning to their left toward second).

OVERTHROW: When a ball is thrown inaccurately to a base and goes into foul territory. The ball is usually played as a live ball in play. But if it is blocked by going into a dugout or under a fence, runners are usually allowed to advance two more bases.

PICKUP GAME: A loosely organized game that generally happens because someone has found enough players to divide up into two teams and play.

PINCH HITTER: A substitute batter who often stays in the field for the rest of the game.

PIVOT FOOT: A foot that the pitcher keeps in constant contact with the pitching rubber until the ball is released. A ball may be called if this is not done correctly.

PROTEST: An assertion by either team that either a playing rule has been misinterpreted or the correct rule has not even been applied by the umpire, or that the correct penalty has not been given by the umpire for a violation. It usually costs money to make a protest to a league to reverse the decision of the umpire, and protests seldom work. If one is upheld, the game may be replayed from that point on or the league may change the decision as to who is the winner.

PULL HITTER: A person who gets maximum power by striking the ball after the wrists have "snapped," thus driving the ball into the "near" field (left field for a right-handed batter).

QUICK PITCH: When a pitcher quickly makes another pitch to the catcher after having just caught the ball returned from the catcher after the preceding pitch. It is designed to catch the batter unaware or off balance. If the umpire declares that it is a "quick pitch," it counts as no pitch. In many cases, however, it is not called and many pitchers use it very effectively.

RALLY: A sudden spurt of improvement in a team's performance.

RBI: A shortened terminology for "runs batted in." An RBI is credited to the batter when a base runner eventually scores as a result of the batter's hit, sacrifice, walk, or even a put out that scores a run.

RELAY: The act of returning the ball from the outfield to the infield by using quick short throws rather than one long throw from the outfielder to a base area. Usually the shortstop or second baseman goes into the outfield to take the relay throw.

SACRIFICE FLY: A ball that is caught before either the first or second out and is deep enough to allow a base runner to score.

SHUT OUT: A game in which one of the teams fails to score.

SMOTHERING THE BALL: To hold on to the ball by covering it with a glove and body rather than catching it cleanly.

SQUIB HIT: A ball hit off of the end of the bat. It may be difficult to field as it often has much spin and wobble on it.

STEALING A BASE: The act of a base runner trying to advance to another base during a pitch to the batter. It is illegal in slow-pitch softball.

STRAIGHT AWAY: Defensively, it refers to the normal position of the team in the field when each player would be in the usual fielding area for that position, rather than shifting to the right or to the left. Offensively, it refers to hitting out toward the center field area.

STREAK HITTER: A batter who is inconsistent offensively and tends to get a string of hits followed by a string of outs.

STRIKE ZONE: In slow-pitch, it is the space over any part of home plate which is between the batter's high shoulder and knees when the batter assumes a natural batting stance. In fast-pitch, it is the space over home plate between the batter's armpits and the top of the knees in a natural stance.

SUCKER PITCH: A pitch in which the pitcher makes a maximum amount of pitching motion and yet the ball is thrown very short. Hopefully, the batter will assume it is going to go deeper than it really does, thus causing either an overstride on the pitch or mistiming of the swing.

TAG-UP: The base runner's action of touching a base before going on to the next base. This must be done after a fly ball has been caught or the runner may be put out if he or she is tagged out before returning to base, or if the defensive player touches this base with the ball in his possession before the runner returns to it.

TALLY: A run scored.

TEXAS LEAGUER: A blooper.

THREE-BAGGER: A hit which allows the batter to reach third base; a triple.

TIME: Another term for "time-out." It can only be called by the umpire though it may be requested by the players.

TOP: Hitting the very top portion of the ball, while swinging naturally. This usually results in a weak ground ball that may catch the defense off-guard.

TRAP: To catch a ball immediately after it starts up from the first bounce.

TRIPLE PLAY: A continuous action play during which three offensive players are put out.

TWO-BAGGER: A hit which allows the batter to reach second base safely; a double.

WAITING OUT: An offensive strategy in which a batter refuses to swing at a pitch until a particularly desired pitch occurs, or there is a base on balls (or a strike out if one isn't careful).

WASTE PITCH: A pitch intentionally thrown outside the strike zone, often blatantly so. It is used in an attempt to trick the batter into swinging at a ball that will be difficult to hit. It is usually used only when the pitcher is well ahead on the count.

WHITEWASH: To keep a team from scoring a single run during a game; a shut out; relatively rare in slow-pitch softball.

List of Champions

There are many different championships one can play for in softball, and in order to list all of the teams who have won some category of national championship in fast and slow pitch softball would be a book in itself. However, since the primary focus is on slow-pitch softball, I would like to honor those teams that have won some of the more recognized national championships. I hasten to again emphasize that there are other national championships, and in any one year a champion in another national category (Women's Class A Slow Pitch, or Men's Church Slow Pitch) might arguably be a better team than a champion in one of our listed categories for that year. One thing I am sure of is that each of these teams would soundly whip the Loonies.

Women's Major Slow Pitch

YEAR		Entries
1961	At Cincinnati, OH—Dairy Cottage, Covington, KY	10
1962	At Cincinnati, Ohio—Dana Gardens, Cincinnati, Ohio	20
1963	At Cincinnati, Ohio—Dana Gardens, Cincinnati, Ohio	24
1964	At Omaha, Neb.—Dana Gardens, Cincinnati, Ohio	26
1965	At Omaha, Neb.—Art's Aces, Omaha, Neb.	31
1966	At Burlington, NC—Dana Gardens, Cincinnati, Ohio	32
1967	At Sheboygan, WI—Ridge Maintenance, Cleveland, Ohio	36
1968	At Cincinnati, Ohio—Escue Pontiac, Cincinnati, Ohio	40
1969	At Chattanooga, TN—Converse Dots, Hialeah, Fla.	47
1970	At Parma, Ohio—Rutenschroer Floral, Cincinnati, Ohio	52
1971	At Satellite Beach, Fla.—Gators, Ft. Lauderdale, Fla.	56
1972	At York, PA—Riverside Ford, Cincinnati, Ohio	32
1973	At Chattanooga, TN—Sweeney Chevrolet, Cincinnati, OH	34
1974	At Elk Grove, CA—Marks Bros., No. Miami Dots, Miami, Fla.	34
1975	At Jacksonville, Fla.—Marks Bros., No. Miami Dots, Miami, Fla.	34
1976	At Chattanooga, TN—Sorrento's Pizza, Cincinnati, OH	33
1977	At Graham, NC—Fox Valley Lassies, St. Charles, ILL.	40
1978	At Jacksonville, Fla.—Bob Hoffman's Dots, Miami, Fla.	41
1979	At Nashville, TN—Bob Hoffman's Dots, Miami, Fla.	39
1980	At York, PA—Howard's Rubi-Otts, Graham, NC	40
1981	At Austin, MN—Tifton Tomboys, Tifton, GA	38
1982	At Marietta, GA—The Stompers, Richmond, VA	39

Men's 16"—Slow Pitch

YEAR		Entries
1964	At Chicago, IL—Bobcats, Chicago, IL	12
1965	At Chicago, IL—Bobcats, Chicago, IL	10
1966	At Chicago, IL—Sobies, Chicago, IL	10
1967	At Chicago, IL—Sobies, Chicago, IL	14

1968	At St. Louis, MO—Sobies, Chicago, IL	15
1969	At Sheboygan, WI—Dr. Carlucci Bobcats, Fox Lake, IL	17
1970	At Waukegan, IL—Dr. Carlucci Bobcats, Fox Lake, IL	16
1971	At Florissant, MO—Dr. Carlucci Bobcats, Fox Lake, IL	21
1972	At Florissant, MO—Dr. Carlucci Bobcats, Fox Lake, IL	23
1973	At Florissant, MO—Dr. Carlucci Bobcats, Fox Lake, IL	27
1974	At Dalton, GA—Strikers, Chicago, IL	29
1975	At Marshalltown, IA—Josef's Chicago, IL	24
1976	At Sioux Falls, S.D.—Dr. Carlucci Bobcats, Chicago, IL	27
1977	At St. Louis, MO—Bobcats, Chicago, IL	28
1978	At Prescott, AZ—Bobcats, Chicago, IL	32
1979	At Harvey, IL—Bobcats, Chicago, IL	24
1980	At Marshalltown, Iowa—Har-Crest Whips, Chicago, IL	30
1981	At Harvey, IL—Budweiser, Harvey, IL	29
1982	At Aberdeen—S.D. Park Avenue Spats, Chicago, IL	28

Men's Major Industrial Slow Pitch

Year		Entries
1957	At Toledo, OH—Turbine Jets, Cincinnati, OH	19
1958	At Cleveland, OH—Turbine Jets, Cincinnati, OH	22
1959	AT Cleveland, OH—Turbine Jets, Cincinnati, OH	26
1960	At Louisville, KY—Pharr Yarn, McAdenville, NC	26
1961	At Toledo, OH—Pharr Yarn, McAdenville, NC	29
1962	At Pittsburgh, PA—Tirabassi Excavt. Kenosha, WI	28
1963	At Providence, RI—Pharr Yarn, McAdenville, NC	34
1964	At Jones Beach, NY—Pabst-International Harvester, Springfield, MO	30
1965	At Detroit, MI—E.L. Wiegand Co., Pittsburgh, PA	34
1966	At McAdenville, NC—IBM, Lexington, KY	35
1967	At Jones Beach, NY—Grumman Aircraft, Bethpage, NY	34
1968	At Stratford, CT—Avco Lycoming, Stratford, CT	36
1969	At McAdenville, NY—Avco Lycoming, Stratford, CT	40
1970	At Jones Beach, NY—Pharr Yarn, McAdenville, NC	38
1971	At York, PA—Pharr Yarn, McAdenville, NC	39
1972	At Providence, RI—Pharr Yarn, McAdenville, NC	42
1973	At McAdenville, NC—Pabst-International Harvester, Springfield, MO	52
1974	At Charlotte, NC—Aetna Life & Casualty, Charlotte, NC	50
1975	At York, PA—Nassau Co. Police Dept., Mineola, NY	32
1976	At Providence, RI—Armco Triangles, Middletown, OH	29
1977	At Birmingham, AL—Armco Triangles, Middletown, OH	34
1978	At Charlotte, NC—GE-Wacos, Louisville, KY	35
1979	At Jacksonville, FL—Sikorsky, Stratford, CT	34
1980	At Lubbock, TX—Sikorsky Aircraft, Stratford, CT	33

| 1981 | At Moultrie, GA—Raffield Fisheries, Port St. Joe, FL | 35 |
| 1982 | At Kansas City, KN—Sikorsky Aircraft, Stratford, CT | 34 |

Women's Major Industrial Slow Pitch

YEAR		Entries
1979	At St. Louis, MO—Phillip Morris, Richmond, VA	22
1980	At Cleveland, TN—Provident Vets, Chattanooga, TN	31
1981	At Birmingham, AL—Provident Vets, Chattanooga, TN	25
1982	At Omaha, NEB—Provident Vets, Chattanooga, TN	28

Men's Super Slow Pitch

YEAR		Entries
1981	At Burlington, NC—Howard's Western Steer, Denver, NC	17
1982	At Burlington, NC—Jerry's Catering, Miami, FL	10

Men's Major Slow Pitch

YEAR		Entries
1953	At Cincinnati, Ohio—Shields Contractors, Newport, KY	12
1954	At Louisville, KY—Waldeck's Tav., Cincinnati, OH	18
1955	At Pittsburgh, PA—Lang's Pet Shop, Covington, KY	24
1956	At Cleveland, Ohio—Gatliff Auto Sales, Newport, KY	26
1957	At Toledo, Ohio—Gatliff Auto Sales, Newport, KY	30
1958	At Cleveland, Ohio—East Side Sports, Detroit, Mich.	32
1959	At Cleveland, Ohio—Yorkshire Rest., Newport, KY	40
1960	At Toledo, Ohio—Hamilton Tailoring, Cincinnati, OH	32
1961	At Louisville, KY—Hamilton Tailoring, Cincinnati, OH	38
1962	At Cleveland, Ohio—Skip Hogan A.C., Pittsburgh, PA	43
1963	At Jones Beach, NY—Gatliff Auto Sales, Newport, KY	46
1964	At Springfield, Ohio—Skip A.C., Pittsburgh, PA	50
1965	At Maumee, Ohio—Skip A.C., Pittsburgh, PA	54
1966	At Parma, Ohio—Michael's Lounge, Detroit, Mich.	62
1967	At Parma, Ohio—Jim's Sport Shop, Pittsburgh, PA	29
1968	At Jones Beach, NY—County Sports, Levittown, NY	28
1969	At Parma, Ohio—Copper Hearth, Milwaukee, WI	34
1970	At Southgate, Mich.—Little Caesar's Southgate, Mich.	32
1971	At Parma, Ohio—Pile Drivers, Virginia Beach, VA	32
1972	At Jacksonville, Fla.—Jiffy Club, Louisville, KY	33
1973	At Cleveland, Ohio—Howard Furniture, Denver, NC	34
1974	At York, PA—Howard Furniture, Denver, NC	34
1975	At Cleveland, Ohio—Pyramid Cafe, Lakewood, Ohio	34
1976	At Jacksonville, Fla.—Warren Motors, Jacksonville, Fla.	33
1977	At Parma, Ohio—Nelson Painting, Okla. City, Okla.	41
1978	At Sacramento, Ca.—Campbell's Carpets, Concord, CA	37
1979	At York, Pa—Nelco Manufacturing, Okla City, Okla.	40

1980	At Montgomery, AL—Campbell's Carpets, Concord, CA	38
1981	At Burlington, NC—Elite Coatings, Gordon, GA	37
1982	At Parma, OH—Triangle Sports, Minneapolis, MN	38

Bibliography

References

Claflin, E. *The Irresistible American Softball Book,* New York: Dolphin Books, 1978.

Cratty, B. *Psychology in Contemporary Sport: Guidelines for coaches and athletes.* Englewood Cliffs, N.J.: Prentice-Hall, 1983.

Fisher, K. Sport psychology comes of age in the '80s. *American Psychological Association Monitor.* 1982, *13 (Sept.),* 1, 8-9, 13.

Hooks, Gene. *Weight Training in Athletics and Physical Conditioning.* Englewood Cliffs, N.J.: Prentice-Hall, 1974.

Croce, P. *Stretching for Athletics.* 2nd Edition. West Point, N.Y.: Leisure Press, 1983.

Jacobson, E. *Anxiety and Tension: A physiologic approach.* Philadelphia: J.B. Lippincott, 1964.

Kavner, R., & Dusky, L. *Total Vision,* Reading, Mass.: Addison-Wesley, 1978.

Marr, D. *Vision,* San Francisco: W.S. Freeman, 1982.

Mentzer, M., & Friedberg, A. *Mike Mentzer's Complete Book of Weight Training,* N.Y.: William Morrow, 1982.

Meyer, R. *The Clinician's Handbook.* Boston: Allyn & Bacon, 1983.

Mirkin, G., & Hoffman, M. *The Sportsmedicine Book,* Boston: Little Brown, 1978.

Murrary, J., & Karpovich, P. *Weight training in Athletics,* Englewood Cliffs, N.J.: Prentice-Hall, 1982.

Nideffer, R. *The Ethics and Practice of Applied Sports Psychology,* Ithaca, New York: Mouvment Publications, 1981.

Noren, A. *Softball,* New York: A.S. Barnes, 1947.

Pesmen, C. The athletic eye. *Esquire,* 1983, *93(3)* 19-21.

Peterson, J. *Total Fitness: The Nautilus Way.* 2nd Edition. West Point, N.Y.: Leisure Press, 1983.

Reichler, J.(Ed.) *The Baseball Encyclopedia.* New York: MacMillan, 1982.

Slote, J. The social sport. *Esquire,* 1982, *July,* 17-18.

Stein, H. The glory boys. *Esquire,* 1981, *Feb.,* 36-48.

Suinn, R. (Ed.) *Psychology in Sports.* Minneapolis, Minn.: Burgess, 1980.

Tutko, T. *Sports Psyching,* Los Angeles, J.P. Tarcher, 1976.

Books for the Spirit

Angell, R. *Late Innings.* N.Y.: Simon & Schuster, 1982.

Boswell, T. *How Life Imitates the World Series.* Garden City, N.Y.: Doubleday, 1982.

Claflin, E. *The Irresistible American Softball Book.* New York: Dolphin Books, 1978.

Kinsella, W. *Shoeless Joe.* Boston: Houghton-Mifflin, 1982.

Leonard, G. *The Ultimate Athlete.* New York: Viking Press, 1975.

Luciano, R., & Fisher, D. *The Umpire Strikes Back.* New York: Bantam, 1982.

Stein, H. The glory boys. *Esquire,* 1981, *Feb.,* 36-48.

Slote, J. The social sport. *Esquire,* 1982, *July,* 17-18.

Uecker, B., & Herskowitz, M. *Catcher in the Wry.* New York: G.B. Putnam's Sons, 1982.

About the Author

Robert G. Meyer, Ph.D. has played, coached and managed both slow and fast pitch softball teams for men, coed and women teams. Dr. Meyer grew up in the 40's and 50's in the Northern Kentucky and Cincinnati areas, the source of many slow pitch champions during those eras. He later played and coached in Chicago, the home of softball, as well as in Michigan, Indiana, California, and North Carolina. When not playing softball, he is a professor of clinical and forensic psychology at the University of Louisville, and has published some 40 plus articles and three books (*Abnormal Psychology, The Clinician's Handbook, Case Studies in Abnormal Psychology*) in psychology. He has served as a consultant and has published in the areas of sports psychology, hypnosis, biofeedback, and stress management.